The Moonlighters

The Moonlighters

*A fictional account of
Central Oregon's Vigilante Years
1882—1884*

By the Author of *Wasco*

Martel Scroggin

Binford & Mort Publishing
Portland, Oregon

The Moonlighters

Copyright © 1992 by Martel Scroggin

Printed in the United States of America

Library of Congress Catalog Card Number: 92-71415

ISBN: 0-8323-0496-4

First Edition 1992

For Gretchen

and all the Joyce Howards, Nancy Carolls and Mary Kays
whose deaths seem so senseless.

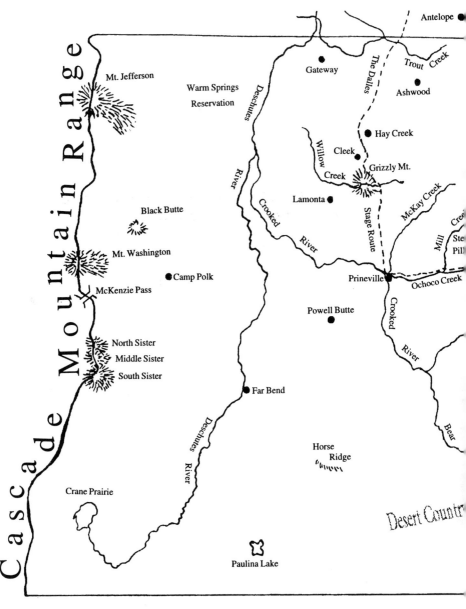

Crook County —1883

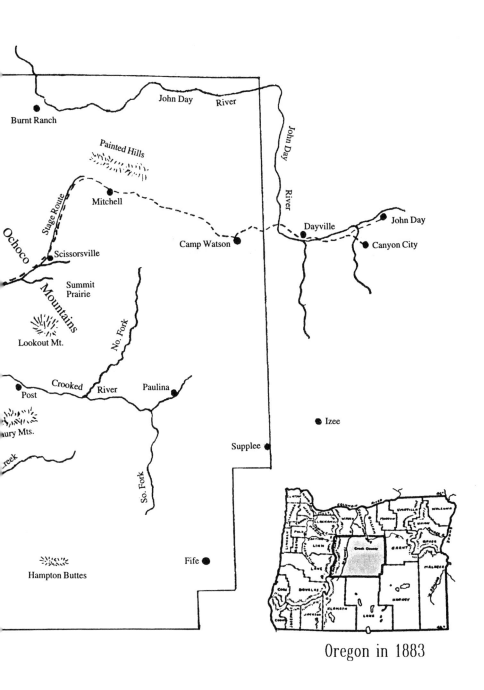

Burnt Ranch

John Day River

Painted Hills

Mitchell

Stage Route

Ochoco

Scissorsville

Mountains

Summit Prairie

Lookout Mt.

No. Fork

Camp Watson

John Day River

Dayville

John Day

Canyon City

Crooked River

Post

Paulina

Izee

...ury Mts.

...reek

Supplee

So. Fork

Hampton Buttes

Fife

Oregon in 1883

Author's note:

The word *Ochoco* is an Indian word meaning "willows."
It is pronounced Ō-chuh-kō.

CHAPTER ONE

March, 1882

Patches of frozen snow spotted the dark, sage-covered ground. Above, grey-bottomed clouds formed a somber pattern in the icy blue sky and cast their slow moving shadows on the desolate landscape. Garrett Maupin shuddered as a sudden gust of chill wind pierced his thin frame. He hunched lower in the saddle and adjusted the frayed and worn Indian blanket that covered his neck and shoulders.

When Maupin reached the rutted stage road that ran from Shaniko past Grizzly Peak, he stopped to roll a smoke. His movements were unhurried as he took a wooden sulphur match from his pocket and lit it with the work-roughened nail of his right thumb. Cupping his hands to keep the fire alive, he bent his head and touched the flame to the tip of his cigarette. The twisted end of paper caught, flared, then reached the tobacco. He inhaled deeply. As pungent smoke circled his face, Maupin's thoughts drifted to the country that surrounded him and how it had grown. It didn't seem possible that over six hundred people lived in the area now; an area bounded by The Dalles to the north, Prineville to the south, east by the Ochoco Mountains and west by Crooked River. Just fifteen years ago he could have counted the number of families who had settled in this section of Wasco County on the fingers of his two hands.

Maupin's parents had been among the first immigrants to arrive in Central Oregon. Like most early

1

settlers, they came from the Willamette Valley. The first years weren't easy and were spent fighting Indians, starvation and brutal winters before they were able to gain a foothold in this hard, unforgiving land.

It was Garrett's father Howard who had killed and scalped the renegade Paiute chief Pe-le-nie. The white pioneers, finding it hard to imitate the guttural Indian pronunciation, called him Paulina.

The killing of Paulina was quite a story. One told and retold by every family in the Ochocos. Howard Maupin, who operated a stage relay station, had been alerted by Jim Clark, a stagecoach driver who saw a band of Indians pushing several head of cattle taken from Andrew Clarno's ranch at John Day. Maupin, Clark and Maupin's neighbor, Bill Ragan, tracked the raiders throughout the night. Early the next morning Maupin and his companions spotted the Indians in a high-walled basalt canyon by Trout Creek. The hostiles were feasting on a butchered steer. From a vantage point on the rimrocks above, Maupin raised his Henry rifle, picked a tall, scarred Indian standing by the fire and pulled the trigger. His aim was true and the Indian fell to the ground. At the sound of the shot, the rest of the band jumped on their horses and fled. After taking the scalp of the Indian he had killed, Maupin and his companions collected Clarno's stock and turned back. They left the body of the dead Indian unburied, a gift for the coyotes and scavenging buzzards that were already circling in the windless sky.

Days later, after word had been spread by the renegades who escaped, Howard Maupin learned whom he had killed. People came from miles around to see Paulina's scalp, which was still drying on the outside wall of the Maupin cabin.

As Garrett Maupin relaxed with his tobacco, he recalled an earlier incident that had almost resulted in his own death. His father's stage station in Antelope had been raided by Paulina, who stole their stock of horses. Howard Maupin was hopping mad and took out after them alone. Before he left he told his wife to keep their twelve-year-old son Garrett in the house. Despite the warning, Garrett sneaked out to follow his father. The elder Maupin, hearing a horse behind him, laid in wait. His finger was tightening on the trigger when he heard a jangling noise. Only days before he had given his son a knife on a chain that made the same sound. He called out, "Goddamnit, Garrett, is that you?" Garrett quickly replied, "It's me, Pa," then got the worst tongue-lashing he could remember ever receiving from his father.

Garrett Maupin grinned at this memory, took one last pull on his cigarette, spat in his glove, ground it out and dropped it to the ground.

He was unwrapping the reins from the saddle horn to continue his journey when three shots echoed from a pine-studded valley to his left. The flat crack of each round told Maupin they came from one of the newer cartridge rifles. A percussion weapon would have made a solid boom.

"Those came from over by Langdon's place, Ted," he spoke aloud to his horse. "Must be Lucius shooting some game." Patting the neck of his mount he added, "We haven't talked to anyone in a spell. Let's drop by and say hello." At the sound of his name the horse pricked up both ears and replied with a whinny and a shake of his head.

Garrett turned in the direction the shots came from and carefully picked his way through the sharp, lava rock sage. As he reached the ridge that separated Lucius Langdon's property from that of his neighbor Aaron Crooks and Crooks's son-in-law, Steve Jory, it entered his mind that Langdon's wife just might ask him to stay for a bite to eat. She had the reputation of being one of the best cooks in the community of Grizzly and the prospect of a home-cooked meal was a pleasant thought. Garrett

3

Maupin had left his spread near Antelope at first light after a hasty breakfast of cold coffee and hard biscuits, all that was left to eat in his small bachelor cabin. That's why he was on his way to Prineville, to load up on supplies.

As he plodded along, Garrett wondered how Lucius, known for his quick temper, was getting along with his neighbors. It was common knowledge that they were at odds over the property line that separated their two places. Crooks wanted to put a cabin on another 160 acres of homestead land in his son-in-law's name; land that Crooks would control. Crooks's daughter Melinda and her husband Steve Jory were living in the same crowded shack that Crooks and his wife Anna shared with their five other children. Melinda was six months pregnant and Aaron Crooks felt it was time they had their own place.

The dispute about the property line had taken a violent and bitter turn. Most people, not knowing who was right, had avoided taking sides.

Last spring, a year ago, Langdon had filed under the Preemptive Law Act that gave a squatter the right to purchase, for $1.25 an acre, the land on which he had settled. In August, five months later, Crooks filed on a section that overlapped Langdon's land. He had filed under the General Preemption Act, another law that allowed squatters to use either surveyed or non-surveyed public land. Langdon had made several trips to the Land Office at The Dalles to protest Crooks's claim. An investigation was underway and a decision was pending in the Wasco County courthouse at The Dalles.

The fact that one of them would lose only aggravated the situation. There was talk that a number of prominent stockmen were siding with Crooks because they thought Lucius Langdon and his brother Al were rustling horses. Garrett had heard the rumor but discounted it. He knew

4

Lucius was honest and hard working, barely able to scratch a living off his claim. He wasn't so sure about Al, though. Al ran with a tough bunch, and was never around to attend to his chores at his ranch on Mill Creek. Also, Al always seemed to have plenty of cash as well as horses to sell or trade.

In any case, it's none of my business, Garrett reminded himself.

Garrett had been engrossed in these thoughts, not paying much attention when suddenly, a hundred yards to his left, a fast moving white horse crashed out of a dense stand of jack pine, scrambled to gain a foothold on a cut bank, and disappeared into heavier timber. It was heading east at a dead run. Through a break in the trees, Maupin saw the rider holding a Winchester repeating rifle in his right hand.

Maupin cautiously kneed his horse forward. He kept to the shadow-filled side of a steep draw and worked his way slowly toward the spiral of grey smoke that marked the location of the Langdon cabin. With as much rustling as had been going on lately, it was best to take no chances.

The buzzing whine of excited flies reached his ears before he spotted the two bodies. They were lying by a line of trees that had been recently blazed. Beads of pine sap still glistened from the freshness of their cut.

One crumpled form was face up; the other face down, arms outstretched. Maupin quickly dismounted and bent over the body nearest him. It was Aaron Crooks. Crooks had been shot through the chest and shoulder. His grey eyes stared unseeing at the now churning dark clouds in the sky above. By his hand was a woodsman's heavy, single blade timber axe. Maupin hurried to the man who was sprawled face down. The sour taste of bile burned the back of his throat as he saw a swarm of blue-green blowflies feasting on the gaping hole in the man's back.

5

Brushing them away with his hat, he rolled the lifeless figure over. It was Crooks's son-in-law, Steve Jory.

Garrett Maupin hurriedly remounted and raced to the Langdon cabin. As he pulled up in front of the unpeeled log and mud-chinked building, he saw Mrs. Langdon standing in the open doorway. She was nervously twisting her apron. Tears coursed down her cheeks and her eyes were wide in shock. As Maupin pulled to a stop, she stared at him and, in a voice hoarse with emotion said, "They shouldn't have done it. They shouldn't have been cuttin' their boundaries on our property."

She reached toward Maupin as if to touch him, but her hand stopped in mid-air. Her voice cracked. "He didn't mean to kill them. He told me. Something just snapped." Then again she repeated, her voice dropping to a whisper, "They just shouldn't have been marking our trees."

Maupin stared at her for a moment, wondering what to do next. Then he made his decision. He spurred his horse as he headed back toward the stage road and swung south. There was nothing he could do here. This was a matter for Deputy Sheriff John Ericksen in Prineville.

CHAPTER TWO

As Garrett Maupin was racing to town to spread the news that Crooks and Jory had been killed, a meeting was taking place at West Fourth and Claypool Streets at the home of Major Sidney "Sid" Duncan.

Eight men were seated around Duncan's eagle claw dining room table.

Some were sprawled in relaxed comfort, others sat easily with their elbows or arms on the polished black surface. One was seated at rigid attention with arms folded. This was Major Duncan. Clockwise from Major Duncan sat County Judge C. E. Duncan who had been appointed two years ago by the recently replaced governor LaFayette Grover, a Democrat. Previously, he had represented Wasco County as a state senator during the Bannock Indian War. Unlike his brother Sid, who was slightly built and had a wispy Custer-style mustache, C. E. was portly and florid faced. A bushy, well-groomed walrus mustache hung over his full upper lip. He outweighed his brother by a good fifty pounds and stood three inches taller.

Sitting at C. E. Duncan's left was Gus Brinkley, a nervous sparrow-like man whose darting eyes never seemed to rest. Brinkley was narrow shouldered and cadaverously thin. There was an inch gap between his neck and celluloid collar, and his coat gave the appearance of being two sizes too large. Brinkley owned one of the largest mercantile stores in town.

7

Next to Brinkley was John Ericksen, Prineville's Deputy Sheriff. By Ericksen was Bill Bernhart, Wasco County Deputy Marshal. Bernhart, broad-shouldered and muscular, was also the town blacksmith.

After Bernhart came Charley Conwell. Conwell had served as a scout for the Army during the Modoc and Bannock Indian wars. The whites of his eyes were dulled a permanent red which was the result of his putting chewing tobacco under his lids to stay awake during the three days and nights it took him to track and kill one of the Snake leaders of the '78 Bannock uprising. Conwell was currently employed by the Duncan brothers, who owned a ranch on Willow Creek, north of Prineville, near Grizzly Mountain. Although he drew a salary as a ranch hand, Conwell never bothered with ranch duties.

Sam Richards faced Gus Brinkley across the table. Richards was a school teacher and served also as Justice of the Peace for Prineville. His wedge-shaped face and pointed dimpled chin were crowned by a ring of light brown hair that surrounded a pink, premature bald spot. He was 27. The youngest person there.

Sitting next to Richards, and to the right of Sid Duncan, was Richards's brother-in-law George Cotter. Cotter, a dark-eyed intense man, had a face so pockmarked and pitted that no razor could ever reach all of the whiskers of his coal-black stubble. George was the son of Origen Cotter, one of the first pioneers to settle in the Ochocos. He was also the town's first, and only, attorney.

There was one member of the group that was not present: B. F. Alben, the town banker. Alben was busy foreclosing on a mortgage, and had sent word he would be there, but would arrive late.

There were several reasons for this meeting. Central Oregon was being plagued by a rash of horse and cattle rustling. The people seated around the ornate walnut table were there to discuss the formation of a stock association that would be structured to accomplish two things: stop the rustling, and keep sheep out of the Ochoco and Crooked River grasslands. Equally important, they were all acutely aware that, next November, a new county was to be carved out of vast Wasco County, a county that covered all land in Oregon east of the Cascade Mountains. They were all politically active and wanted to be sure the current Governor, W. W. Thayer, a Democrat, would make an effort to appoint them to positions of power before the general election of county officers that would be held after the new county was established. One of their goals was to make Prineville the county seat. Other cities vying for this honor were Cleek, Mitchell and nearby Mill Creek.

Sid Duncan, the group's organizer, had acquired the title of Major during the Modoc Indian War when he acted as a personal representative and liaison between Governor LaFayette Grover—the man who had appointed his brother judge—and the Army. An editorial in the *Portland Oregonian* referred to Duncan as "the governor's mad-cap Major." Even though the article was not a complimentary one, and the military designation was made in jest, Sid Duncan accepted the rank and from that day on referred to himself as Major Duncan.

Sid Duncan, unlike his brother C.E., was short-tempered and violent. As editor and publisher of the weekly paper in Roseburg, he killed two brothers who had publicly disagreed with an editorial he had written. During the gunfight he was shot twice. One of the bullets lodged behind and below his jawbone, which left him with a permanently stiff neck. He often proudly pointed out the lump at the back of his head to show that the bullet was still there.

It was Major Duncan who spoke first. "Gentlemen, thank you for coming." He cleared his throat, pulled at one of his overly large ears then chewed one end of his

9

sparse mustache. "John and Bill," he nodded at the two law officers, "have just returned from The Dalles where they had a session with Sheriff Storrs. Storrs said he sympathized with our rustling problem, but he just doesn't have enough manpower to cover a county two-thirds the size of the state. He gave full authority to Deputy Sheriff Ericksen to do what was necessary. All he asked was that he be kept informed."

With a chuckle the Major concluded, "I guess that's what we wanted to hear. Any action on our part will have the full sanction of the law. Any comments?"

His brother C. E. responded. "It means we better get to work. First we need to organize the ranchers. Of course," he said with a knowing look at the rest, "the ranchers we'll organize will be those that are head-quartered in what will be the new county." He paused, looked around the table and continued, giving them some news they were unaware of. "The state legislature has decided to call the new county Crook, after Major General George Crook."

Gus Brinkley responded to this news with a snort and a malicious grin aimed at George Cotter. "I thought for sure they would have named it Cotter County, on account of your daddy, George."

George Cotter sent a spiteful glare at the storekeeper. "You can joke about it Gus, but they should have," he said bitterly. "If it weren't for Pa, there would be no Prineville and everybody here knows that."

In 1867, George's father Origen came over the Santiam Pass from Lebanon with five companions. That first year they were burned out by Indians. Left with nothing, Origen Cotter and his group whittled fake rifles out of wood to fool the savages and marched to the Warm Springs Military Post forty miles away. Origen returned the following spring to rebuild. His account of the lush and vast grassland in the Ochocos encouraged more farmers to leave the crowded valley and settle in Central Oregon.

"Now, now," C. E. Duncan interrupted the two men, "the state has already made up its mind." To soothe George he added, "They just might have considered calling it Cotter County, George, but that suit your daddy has with the Willamette Valley and Cascade Mountain Wagon Road Company would have killed it right away. You know how much clout they have with the politicians in Salem. Anyway, as I was saying," he changed the subject, "our first job is to organize the ranchers. With their support, we should have no trouble getting ourselves elected to county office."

"I don't know, C. E.," said Brinkley. "I hear talk in my store. A lot of people don't like the fact some of you were named by a governor who is a Democrat. More and more Republicans are moving into this country to settle."

"Nonsense," Sam Richards interjected. "There's no opposition now, and there's not likely to be any. Who would oppose us? No one wants our jobs. They're too busy trying to scrape a living off the land."

"Sam's right," said Major Duncan. "If we can get the big outfits to pull together and stop all the horse and cattle thieving, they'll look on us as heroes."

George Cotter stood to get everyone's attention. His thin white hands grasped the lapels of his black broadcloth suit. "I've done some preliminary work already. Only three outfits have agreed to support a stock association. Most of the others say they can handle the problem themselves, like they always have. Some are even talking about putting sheep on their land. It's not going to be easy getting them together. Maybe we're just wasting our time."

As Cotter turned to sit down, a low and menacing voice replied. "Maybe there hasn't been enough rustling or sheep killing. Maybe we should just see to it that it's a

11

bigger problem than they think." It was Charley Conwell. After he made this statement, he turned and unleashed a stream of brown tobacco juice at the polished brass spittoon by his chair.

"Charley, as long as you are working for our spread I don't want to hear talk like that in public," C. E. Duncan snapped from his spot at the table.

Charley lifted the palms of both hands, opened his eyes wide and shrugged. "Just talkin' amongst us here, C. E.. For sure something needs to be done to get the local cattlemen off their hind ends."

"Something will be done, Charley," Major Duncan said. The tone of his voice indicated he agreed with Conwell. "I suggest we all sleep on it for a few days and get together again."

The group nodded in agreement. Their chairs scraped the polished pine floor as they stood to leave.

Without warning the door flew open and a white-haired man, who seemed as fragile as the mounted bone china plate on Duncan's sideboard, burst into the room. It was the missing member, banker Benjamin Alben.

He was agitated and excited. The news he brought stunned them all. He looked directly at George Cotter, a slight that Major Sid Duncan didn't miss. Breathlessly Alben blurted out the news he was carrying.

"Garrett Maupin just rode into town. Lucius Langdon shot and killed Aaron Crooks and Steve Jory just a few hours ago. I left Maupin at Burmeister's Saloon. He was looking for you, John," he said, addressing the deputy sheriff.

"In that case, I'd best get down there," said Ericksen. "You better come too, Bill," he said, nodding to Bernhart.

"We'd all better get down there," said George Cotter. "But not in a bunch. Sam, Gus and I will leave by the back door. The rest of you wait a few minutes, then go out the front."

When everyone but the Duncan brothers and Charley Conwell had left, Conwell's sharp black eyes centered on Sid Duncan. He shifted his wad of tobacco, then spoke out. "Major, it looks like the something I said needed to be done to get the ranchers around here off their hinders just happened. With a little help from us, of course," he added. An evil smile lit his hawk-like face.

CHAPTER THREE

Garrett Maupin was finishing his story for the second time when Deputy Sheriff John Ericksen and Deputy Marshal Bernhart elbowed their way through the agitated crowd to where Maupin stood by his lathered horse.

"Now then, Garrett," said Ericksen, "What's this I hear about two killings?"

Once again Garrett recounted what he had seen. "It looked like Crooks and Jory had been cutting boundary markers when Langdon shot them down, Sheriff. Then he jumped on his horse and lit out. The last I saw, he was headed east, toward Mill Creek."

"Probably to his brother's place," boomed out a voice. It was Major Duncan, who had just arrived with his brother and Charley Conwell. Duncan, erect and stiff-necked, took charge immediately. "We had better gather up a posse to get him, Sheriff." Picking out three men, who minutes earlier had been sitting around his dining room table, Duncan called out their names. "George, Charley, Sam. Let's get over to the stable and saddle up. Sheriff, you stay here in case Langdon comes to town."

As the four started to move out, a voice spoke up. "Think I might join you." It was Gil Wayne, the owner of one of Prineville's four saloons.

Wayne didn't fit the stereotype of a saloon man. He was big, rawboned and husky. There was seldom any trouble in the Wayne Saloon. Even though Wayne gave the appearance of being mild mannered, his presence and overly-casual comment, "Beat on yourselves outside, but not in here," usually stopped any fights that were about to develop in his bar. In The Dalles he had killed the two Whitley brothers in a showdown on Main Street. The gun he used was prominently hung behind the bar in his saloon. He often referred to it affectionately as 'old Whit', and said he wouldn't hesitate to use it again if he ever had to.

The fact that Wayne had volunteered to join them made Duncan uneasy. He didn't know where Wayne stood in regard to the town's politics and he would have preferred to have men with him that were under his control.

Duncan paused, then addressed Wayne. "Gil, we appreciate your offer of help, but we probably should send a group to Langdon's place in case he doubles back. Why don't you handle that?"

Wayne's answer irritated Major Duncan, who struggled to keep his anger from showing. "Major," said Wayne, "I see Bill Russell over there. He knows Lucius and his family. Let Bill go, and take some people to back him up. I'll stick with you."

Resigned to the fact that he couldn't shake Wayne, Duncan nodded curtly. "Fine." Then, realizing that further delay might mean more people would want to join his small band he said brusquely, "We're wasting time. Let's hit the trail," and hurried away.

Although Bill Russell was only 30 years old, he commanded the respect of someone much older. Thin, homely, ramrod straight and ham-fisted, Russell had arrived in Prineville from Brownsville fifteen years ago after he had driven some beef cattle to California. Russell had a working ranch on Willow Creek, not far from the Duncan brothers. And, like the Duncans, lived in town with a younger brother. In fact, he lived on Claypool across the street from Sid Duncan's home. One of eleven children,

Russell was a seasoned cowman long before many of his friends had made the decision whether to go on to high school or go to work.

In a quiet, measured voice, Russell spoke out. "Seems to me, Sheriff, you should be the one heading up any posse. You or Bill there," he said, indicating Deputy Marshal Bernhart. "Not Duncan or me."

Put on the spot, the deputy's cheeks reddened. He blurted out a reply. "I got too much work to do here to leave. I was going to suggest someone else head up a posse, but the Major beat me to it."

With a touch of sarcasm in his voice, Russell squinted and stared hard at the lawman. "We know how busy you are, John. How about the Deputy Marshal going?" He nodded again at Bill Bernhart.

"Not in my jurisdiction, Bill," Bernhart answered, looking to Deputy Ericksen for support. As he finished his excuse, the hooves of Duncan's departing posse drummed down the street.

Russell's face turned grim. "Well, somebody should check Langdon's place. Duncan is right about that. Guess I'm stuck. Anyone want to go along?"

"I will," a voice spoke up. "Me too," said another. The two men who volunteered were Jim Coggin and Elon Lee, small ranchers from Crooked River Valley. Joe Schoolin, a young ranch hand who worked for Lee said he would tag along too, if it was all right with his boss. Minutes later, at precisely four o'clock, they left, riding north up Main to take the McKay trail to Grizzly; the same route Garrett Maupin had taken when he rode in with the news of the murders.

Major Duncan's party had been riding for more than an hour. No one had spoken since they left Prineville. Each man was wrapped up in his own private thoughts.

Two men in particular were looking beyond what tonight's action would bring: George Cotter and Gil Wayne.

Cotter chuckled silently to himself as he followed Duncan. Let the Major take all the credit and glory, as long as I keep pulling the string, Cotter thought smugly. Duncan was his puppet and both men knew it, but Sid Duncan was too caught up in his own importance to let it bother him. As long as the Major was able to strut and boast, and appear the big dog, he would do the bidding of George Cotter.

Yes, Cotter mused, Duncan is well suited to do the dirty work. Let Duncan stick his neck out. He would stay behind the scenes and could jump whichever way the wind blew. Cotter wasn't so sure Governor Thayer would be re-elected in October. The Major would never change his political stripes, but it didn't matter to Cotter which party was in power—just as long as he landed on the winning side.

Gil Wayne, who tailed the procession, was doing his own planning. When Wayne was bartending his genial manner fronted another purpose. His ambition was to be more than just a saloon keeper. He wanted to be a respected and influential member of the community. Wayne kept abreast of the town's politics. He knew two power groups were taking shape in Central Oregon and these two factions were bound to clash eventually. The more vocal of the two groups was the one he was riding with. The Cotter gang, he called them. Sid Duncan was making all the noise, but he knew who really called the shots. It was George Cotter. These men wanted power and didn't care how they got it. They would smash anyone who got in their way.

On the other side of the coin were a handful of large ranchers, most of the small ranchers, the homesteaders and a majority of Prineville's merchants.

17

As yet, this group was unorganized. But Wayne knew the day would come when they would be forced to band together. He knew who the leaders would be, too: Tom Pickett, Clay Howard and Bill Russell. Pickett was a partner of the 3C ranch, the Columbia Cattle Company, one of the largest spreads in Ochoco Valley. Also, Pickett had a major interest in three important Ochoco gold mines, and one-third interest in a Willamette River steamship line. His influence in the area and with the politicians in Salem was substantial.

Clay Howard, an older rancher, had a large spread on Crooked River but lived in town. Howard was well liked, trusted and respected. When the time came Wayne knew Howard would be the first of the three to make his feelings known.

The third man was Bill Russell, who was leading the other posse.

Wayne doubted that these three men even realized the part they would eventually play. All would have to be forced to it, but there was no question in his mind that it would come about, and that they would respond. In the end there would only be one winner and until Wayne knew who that would be, he intended to straddle the fence. In that respect he was like George Cotter.

Both Cotter's and Wayne's trains of thought were interrupted by Duncan's signal to stop. The riders gathered around the Major. Their horses clouded the group with quick bursts of mist from their nostrils. All but Charley Conwell stood in their saddles to stretch their cramped muscles. The creak of saddle leather cut through the crisp cold of the early evening and blew down Ochoco Creek on a bitter dusk wind. Cotter rubbed his nose and ears vigorously to renew circulation while Sam Richards pulled his hands from his gloves and blew on them. Charley Conwell sat quietly, unaffected by the bitter cold, contemptuous of those who were showing their discomfort.

Duncan issued his orders. "We'll stop at Ewen Johnson's. He knows the country like a book and can tell us what the layout is at Al Langdon's place." Not waiting for a reply, he clicked his tongue and urged his horse forward.

Lantern light from Johnson's shack cut through the night as the posse drifted into an area of stumps that surrounded the small cabin. Johnson appeared at the doorway, holding up a coal-oil lamp in his left hand. A shield on the back of the lamp threw out its glare, catching the group of horsemen.

Johnson was wearing nothing but old felt slippers and heavy woolen long johns which were stained with dirt and food from his bachelor meals. His right hand held a cocked .44-caliber Remington.

"There's nothing to worry about, Ewen," Cotter called out, seeing the gun. "It's George Cotter, Major Duncan and some of the boys from town."

Johnson showed his spirit by cursing and complaining angrily. He ended his tirade with, "The next time you come sneaking up on a man in the middle of the night, call out down the road, else your liable to end up with some holes in your hide."

"Ewen, it's not even seven o'clock yet. How can you say it's the middle of the night," Richards replied jovially.

"To you city slickers it may be early, but I get up and go to bed with the chickens, and they went to bed two hours ago," Johnson snapped back.

The posse dismounted and hurried through the door to the warmth of the smoldering fire in the stone fireplace. Johnson stirred the coals and threw on some dry juniper ends. As they began to blaze, Duncan kneeled to warm his hands and explain what had happened, and why they were there.

19

"Sure I'll join you," Johnson snorted. " I never did care much for Al Langdon. He doesn't like to get his hands dirty like the rest of us. I always figured Lucius was a square shooter though," he added. His brow wrinkled as he thought that statement through. Then he went to a peg in the log wall, took down his overalls, slipped them on and adjusted the straps over his bony shoulders. After that he put on cowhide work boots and went to the fire. He gave the logs a poke with a blackened angle iron to settle them down. "Let's git to gittin'," he said.

"Hold on, Ewen," Duncan replied. "We need to know the layout of Langdon's place. I want to catch Al and Lucius by surprise. I don't want either of them getting away."

"What's to know," Johnson said curtly. "He's half a mile up the road, and his cabin sits by the creek. The land has been cleared around his place, same as mine."

"Is his house backed up to the woods?" Duncan asked.

"I just told you his land had been cleared around his place," Johnson snapped testily.

"All right then, here's our plan," said Duncan. "We'll surround the cabin, call out whoever is inside and shoot them down when they come out."

"Hold on now," sputtered Johnson. "I don't hold with no cold-blooded killings. They ought to at least get their say in court."

"Ewen's right," soothed Cotter. "I think what Sid meant to say, Ewen, was that if they put up a fight we'll have to return fire. Isn't that right, Sid?" Cotter stared meaningfully at Duncan.

"Of course, of course," Duncan blustered. "It just stands to reason that a man who kills two unarmed men won't surrender without a fight."

As they filed out, Duncan held Cotter back and whispered fiercely, " I meant what I said George, and you know it. Just as you know I go by the title of Major."

"Of course I know it, *Major*," Cotter said, emphasizing the title. "But you don't have to tell the world about it. Remember, both Wayne and Johnson are with us."

As the group neared Al Langdon's house and barn, a dog confronted them in the road, barking fiercely. Seconds later, a door opened, throwing lantern light on the ground. Next they heard the pounding of hooves as a horse raced away.

"Let's get him, Gil," yelled Charley Conwell, no longer seeing any need for caution. Both Wayne and Conwell spurred their mounts in pursuit.

"Surround the house," Duncan called out excitedly. "Shoot down anyone who comes out."

As his companions circled the rough hewn cabin, Duncan guided his horse to the dog who had signalled the alarm. Still barking and baring his teeth, the dog backed away. Duncan shot the dog twice. "Damned mouthy mutt," he snarled.

CHAPTER FOUR

"What's going on, Bill?" Joe Schoolin asked Russell when the four-man posse stopped to give their horses a breather.

"What do you mean?" Russell asked, his brow furrowing as he eyed the young ranch hand. "I thought it was obvious. We're headed to Langdon's place to see if he's there."

"I don't mean that," Schoolin replied, holding out a folded piece of paper, "I mean this."

Russell's perpetual frown deepened as he reached out to take the note Schoolin handed him. He read it and snapped angrily, "Where did you get this?"

"Sheriff Ericksen handed it to me, just as we started to leave."

"Have you read it?"

"Yep," Schoolin replied. "But it made no sense to me."

"That's for sure," Russell snorted, as he stuffed the message in his vest pocket. He turned to Coggin and Lee. "It's a warrant from Justice of the Peace Richards. We're supposed to arrest Langdon's hired man, W. H. Harrison, for being an accomplice to the murders."

"But Harrison was in town all day. I saw him myself," Jim Coggin said. His voice echoed his surprise.

"So did I, and so did a lot of others," Russell grunted.

"So, what are we going to do?" Elon Lee asked.

"Nothing," Russell said. "Our job is to bring in Lucius Langdon if we find him, and that's it as far as I'm concerned."

Their approach to Langdon's hand-hewn cabin was marked by the bay of a deep-throated hound. After his short protest the animal trotted amongst the riders. Its tail wagged excitedly. "Hello, Ben," Russell addressed the dog in a friendly manner.

The sun had set an hour ago and twilight was giving way to darkness. They could still see, but barely. Someone was mounted on a white horse in the shadows that enveloped the house.

Russell called out as they rode up. "Is that you, Lucius? It's Bill Russell."

A voice tinged with relief replied. "I thought it looked like you, Bill, but I wasn't sure."

A spare figure got off the white horse and came forward. "At least now I know I'll get a fair shake."

Russell and his men dismounted and wearily trooped into the house where they were met by Mrs. Langdon. She was still on the edge of hysteria, but had not forgotten her frontier manners.

"You folks must be starved. I'll fix something to eat."

"That would be kind of you, Emma," Russell said, noting the black half circles that accentuated her red-rimmed eyes. As he watched her face, a muscle in her jaw twitched nervously. His eyes left her face and he glanced around the room. W. H. Harrison, Langdon's hand, was sitting at a hand-crafted table, with a half-empty plate in front of him. Russell acknowledged him with a nod. "Evenin', W. H."

"Just got here myself," Harrison said uneasily. A cup of coffee was cradled in his hands. "I thought someone should tell Lucius or Emma that a posse was on its way."

Langdon, who had slumped in a rickety pine rocking chair in the corner of the one room cabin, spoke out. His voice was shaky as he picked at the bark that was still stuck to one of the arms. "After the shootin', I went to see my brother Al. He said I should fess-up. He was going to ride to The Dalles with me. I was going to turn myself in to Sheriff Storrs. Then his dog started barking something fierce and we spotted this group of riders out of the window. I panicked I guess, got on my horse and rode home. Two men followed me, but I lost them this side of Green Mountain."

"Lucius, you know we've got to take you in," said Russell. His voice held its normal tone.

Langdon looked up in fright. "Not to Prineville, Bill. They'll kill me. Take me to The Dalles. I know I'll get a fair trial there." His voice ended in a whisper as he pleaded, "But not Prineville."

Harrison stood up and came to where Langdon was sitting. He put a hand on Langdon's shoulder. "Lucius, you've been good to me and my son. Took me in when my wife died and I didn't know what to do. I'll go in with you and stay with you to see that nothing happens. Your brother will come in, too, just as soon as he hears you're in town."

"It's got to be that way, Lucius," Russell said softly. "I give you my word that you'll get a fair trial. As soon as we've had a bite to eat, and after I ride over to tell Mrs. Crooks and Melinda Jory what is happening, we'll have to head to town."

"Bill," Langdon screeched, looking frantically at Russell, then at the rest of the men who came to get him, "you don't understand. Major Duncan wants my land, and if he has to kill me to get it, he will."

24

CHAPTER FIVE

Eight grim-faced men filed through the front door of the dimly lit saloon. The jingle of their spurs jarred the silence as did the squeak of the batwing doors as they swung open and shut. The upright clock in the hotel that adjoined the bar struck four times. Its last toll echoed mournfully through the thin clapboard walls.

The men lined up at the bar. Their leader reached for a bottle which stood beside eight empty glasses that had been left for them.

Nervous tension hung in the air like a shroud. The man who led them in pulled the cork from the bottle with his teeth, spat it out and poured a generous measure of whiskey in each glass.

At his stiff-necked nod, they reached for their drinks, raised their glasses in a silent salute, and downed the fiery liquid. The light from the lone coal oil lamp that hung from a ceiling rafter above them flickered as an early morning breeze rearranged its flame. The sway of the lamp threw surrealistic shadows behind the eight figures who laid their empty glasses back on the counter.

The man who had poured reached inside his shirt and pulled out a flour sack mask which he quickly slipped over his head. The others followed suit. One of the eight, a sparrow-like figure whose eyes darted nervously at each of his companions, was thankful for the dim light that hid the nervous sweat running in rivulets down his face.

They left the saloon as silently as they had entered and walked to the hallway that connected the bar to the

Culver Hotel, the town's only hostelry. After passing the fold-up plank that served as a registration desk, they stepped purposefully up the stained and worn carpet-covered stairs that led to the second floor. The last to follow, his red tinged eyes showing through the slots in his mask, carried a saddle rope. As he walked, he deftly fashioned a hangman's knot.

They stopped before a door that was marked with a white chalked 'X'. The leader motioned to the second man in line who drew his pistol, raised his foot and kicked open the door. He burst into the room, followed by the others.

There were four people inside. One lay sleeping on a sagging spring bed. At the sound of the shattering door, the person on the bed lifted his head and tried to focus his eyes. His brain never had a chance to function as one of the masked men stepped forward and fired three shots—two into his chest and a third in his head.

On the other side of the room, in a corner, a figure was seated in a straight chair. He wore the clothes of a working man; patched overalls, a red wool shirt that was frayed around the cuffs and neck and laced cowhide boots. His eyes were wide open in alarm. His mouth gaped.

The slight man who led the group jerked his head stiffly in the direction of the frightened man and snarled his instructions. "Drag him down the street and hang him from the bridge."

The man in the chair stared back in terror. He was barely able to croak, "You got no cause to bother me." Then, as he saw the noose a rush of adrenalin helped him find his voice. He jumped to his feet and screamed in sheer terror. "Please! I done nothin'! I got a little boy who. . . " The rope cut off his words as he was jerked out of his chair and pulled into the hall.

26

The two other men in the room had been huddled around a pot-bellied stove, trying to absorb its warmth, when the masked men broke in. They both wore badges. The masked leader remained behind as the others left with their victim. He holstered his Colt, walked to the window, pulled back the curtain and watched as the free end of the rope that choked its struggling victim was tied to the saddle horn of a red roan. He nodded with satisfaction as the nervous mare was quirted. Nostril's flaring, the horse bolted down the street, dragging it's bouncing bundle behind.

Turning, he faced the lawmen and pulled off his hood. "Well, Sheriff," Major Duncan said. "It looks like I'd better tie you and Bill up. I'll put a pillow cover over your heads. That way you can say we came at you from behind and you never saw a thing."

CHAPTER SIX

"Clay, wake up. Something's going on down by the bridge."

Clay Howard sat bolt upright in bed. At first he was sure the ringing he heard was in his head. Then he realized it came from the bell in the two-story school house on the east bank of Crooked River. He had slept fitfully, dreaming of gunshots and fast galloping riders, who a dozen years ago had been rustling his cattle and those of his neighbors in the Ochoco range.

Anxiously, Ellie called his name again. His brain began to register and his eyes focused on his wife, who was standing by the side of the bed. She was clutching a woolen shawl that had been hastily thrown around her shoulders.

"Clay, there are a lot of people up. Something must have happened."

Clay Howard swung his bare feet onto the drafty plank floor.

"Maybe somebody's house is on fire," he said.

"No," Ellie replied. "I looked out the window. There's no smoke and the fire wagon's not out."

"What time is it?"

"Just dawn."

They quickly dressed and hurried to the front door. As they stepped outside, their nostrils prickled from the cold morning air. A heavy frost covered the ground, and the morning wind from the river carried a chill that made them shiver. They could see people leaving their homes and hurrying toward Crooked River bridge.

Clay took Ellie's arm as they walked briskly toward the river, a few blocks away. At the corner of Second Street Ed Stokes, a neighbor, came running up to them. Before they had a chance to ask what the commotion was all about, he blurted out the news.

"It's W. H. Harrison, Lucius Langdon's hired hand. He's dead. Leo Fried saw the whole thing. The vigilantes did it. They drug him all the way from the hotel and hung him from the bridge. Left him dangling half in and half out of the water!"

"When did it happen?" Clay asked, now fully awake and alert.

"Not long ago. I heard some shots, and by the time I got a light going and to the window there were seven riders going by my place, draggin' a body. Leo told me Langdon was killed, too," Stokes exclaimed.

Clay, who was now standing with his arm around Ellie, felt her shudder. She turned and looked at him. "That poor Mrs. Langdon. Two young children to care for and another on the way. What will she do now?" Her face took on a stricken look as she added, "And Harrison had a child, too."

Clay took Ellie's hand in his own and gently patted it. "Now you go on back, Ellie. There's nothing you can do here," he said soothingly. "I'll see if I can be of any help, then I'll hurry home."

Clay joined the throng of excited townspeople. Four men were struggling with a broken and bloody red-shirted body whose arms and legs had frozen stiff at odd angles.

They were headed for Dick Graham's saloon. Graham was both saloon keeper and undertaker for the town.

By the time they reached Main Street the procession had doubled in number. Occasionally, one or two people would drop out to spread the word to their neighbors who were peering nervously out their windows or standing on their porches, watching anxiously . When they reached the saloon, Graham was waiting. He immediately took charge. "Put him in the back, boys. I'll have to measure him up for a box." Turning to the milling group he said, "Bar's open for them as needs a drink. I'll light up the stove and put on a pot of coffee for the rest."

Two men headed for the bar. The rest split into smaller groups to discuss the meaning of what had happened.

Several minutes later, Major Duncan elbowed his way through the front door, went to a table, pulled out a chair with his boot and climbed onto it. "Listen up," he yelled. When the murmur of voices had died down, he pulled at an ear and continued. "I just got word of the two killings. As most of you know by now, Lucius Langdon was shot to death early this morning and his hired hand W. H. Harrison was hung. Whoever did it overpowered Deputy Sheriff Ericksen and Deputy Marshal Bernhart." He nodded at the two lawmen who had entered with him. "Unfortunately both were taken by surprise and their heads were covered up before they could see who their assailants were."

In the back of the room someone snorted. His comment was loud and clear. "In a pig's eye they don't know who did it."

Duncan glared fiercely at the speaker. It was Al Schwartz, a local rancher. After making a mental note of the man's name, Duncan continued.

"Although we don't approve of the methods these eight masked men took, Langdon would have been tried and hung for murder and rustling anyway." Raising his voice to quiet the protest he knew would follow this statement, he quickly added, "However, trial without jury should not be condoned. Therefore I'm asking Sheriff

Ericksen, Deputy Marshal Bernhart and George Cotter to look into the matter." Before his audience could respond, he stepped down and hurriedly left the building. The two silent lawmen followed.

Clay was standing next to Reub Hassler, a 3C rider who had spent the night in town. Clay gripped Reub's arm.

"I don't like the smell of this, Reub. How do you suppose he knew eight men were involved if Ericksen and Bernhart had their heads covered? Ed Stokes said he counted seven in the bunch that dragged Langdon.

"Tell Tom I'd like to see him as soon as it's convenient for him to come to town. Something's in the wind."

Tom was Tom Pickett. He and his partner Todd Howard jointly owned the 3C, the Columbia Cattle Company. Todd, now living in San Francisco, was Clay Howard's grandson, but the bond between Clay and Tom was stronger than that of just being his grandson's partner. Tom had become Clay's closest and most trusted friend.

As Clay and Reub Hassler were having their private conversation, Leo Fried, the storekeeper who was in his shop earlier than usual to fill an order for the morning stage, and who had seen Harrison dragged from the hotel, was jostled hard as he started to leave the saloon. A piece of paper was thrust in his hand. Due to the press of people surrounding him, Fried couldn't tell who had passed it to him. Once he reached the street, he unfolded the paper to glance at the message inside. After reading it, he leaned weakly against the four-by-four post that supported the awning over Graham's saloon. His face turned ghostly white. His mind and body were frozen in shock. The note had been crudely printed. It read, *"FORGIT WHAT YU SAW OR YU WONT LIV TO SEE YUR FAMLY AGIN."* A skull and crossed bones served as a signature.

CHAPTER SEVEN

Reub Hassler returned to the 3C ranch the afternoon of Harrison's hanging. He went directly to the ranch office where he was told Tom Pickett was checking for strays on the west side of Lookout Mountain. Stopping only long enough for a quick cup of coffee, Reub remounted and kicked his horse into a lope, heading up the trail that led to the ranch's high country pasture.

An hour later he found Tom on a pine-covered slope pushing a cow and two calves downhill.

Reub hailed him as his horse scrambled up the ice-spotted slope that separated them.

"Howdy, Reub. What brings you up here in such an all-fired hurry? A husband of one of those girls that you've been chasing in town after you?"

"Wish that was the case," said Hassler, taking the ribbing. "At my age I would consider it a downright compliment." His grin faded. "Clay said to ask you to see him when it's convenient." Then Reub recounted what had happened to Langdon and Harrison.

Tom nodded grimly. He knew Clay would not have made this request unless he felt it was important. He shaded his eyes and glanced at the position of the sun. "Too late to ride in today. I'll head out at first light. Take care of these lost souls will you, Reub." He jerked his head toward the cattle. "I've got some other chores that need tending to before I leave."

Before dawn, Tom was ready to ride. His route would take him down Ochoco Creek, past Mill Creek and on to the cattle community of Prineville.

When the sun broke over Lookout Mountain, he led his horse out of the corral, adjusted his saddle's cinch and mounted. As he trotted down the mud-frozen road that led away from the 3C outbuildings he scanned the sky, as was his habit each morning. Above the outline of the hills on his right, clouds with black bottoms drifted eastward. Left and to his front, patches of blue appeared. The wind stirred, filling his nostrils with the tang of sage and juniper. A nervous jackrabbit started to cross his path, then scurried back to his hole, not sure whether this early rider posed a threat or not. In the sky a prairie falcon, wings spread, circled lazily, searching for his morning meal. Chipmunks scurried along the tops of dead logs, their tails jerking saucily as they stopped to watch his progress.

If there's a better place to live, I don't know where it is, Pickett mused. He loved this wild and untamed country.

Three miles from Prineville, Tom's gaze centered on a hawk that had taken a position on the top of a dead juniper directly in front of him. Turning his back to the wind, which ruffled his feathers, the hawk cocked his head, left the tall barren tree he had chosen as his roost, and plunged to the ground. As he rose, a small rodent squirmed in his sharp claws. The squeal of the terrified animal cut into the silence of the morning.

The sight of the hawk pouncing on his victim jarred Tom back to reality and why he was leaving his duties at the ranch to see Clay Howard. It seemed a law of nature that the strong always fed off the weak. Should it be that way with people, too? The thought made him uneasy.

The winding valley broadened and below him smoke from a hundred chimneys rose straight up into a windless sky that had now become clear and blue.

As he trotted up to Clay's hitching post, the smell of bacon filled his nostrils. His stomach growled noisily. A grin split his lean, freckled face. He had timed his arrival just right.

Tom had just stepped down from the saddle when Clay Howard appeared at the door. "Tom," his voice boomed out a pleased greeting. "Come on in before we all freeze to death."

They embraced unashamedly, then Clay stepped back and held Tom at arms length. He gave him an appraising look. "It's good to see you. It's been too long," he exclaimed. Putting an arm around Tom's shoulders he guided him to the door. "You're a sight for sore eyes. Do you know it's been almost three months since we last saw you?"

"I know, Clay. Last Christmas Eve to be exact. Ellie stuffed me so full of turkey and rice pudding that I've been trying to work it off ever since."

Clay Howard glanced at Tom's suspendered, slight frame and replied, "Looks to me like you've worked it off and then some."

As they entered the house, he shouted out, "Ellie, we've got company. Better throw a slab of bacon and a dozen eggs in the skillet."

Ellie Howard rushed from the kitchen, wiping her hands on a ruffled calico apron. Tom just had time to brace himself as she threw her arms around him and gave him a crushing hug. "What a pleasant surprise," she said, giving him one more squeeze. "Clay," she turned to her husband. "There's that last jar of spiced peaches in the cold pantry. Would you fetch it, please?"

Tom started to protest but Ellie would have none of it. "Nonsense. I've been saving it for a special occasion, and that's what your visit is."

"Tom, I swear you haven't put on a pound since I've known you," Clay Howard exclaimed as he brought the quart jar in and set it on the table. "What you need is to find some pretty thing and settle down. I used to look like a broomstick, but look what happened to me." He laughed and patted his ample girth.

When they had finished breakfast, Clay turned serious. "I guess Reub told you that I wanted to talk. And I suppose he told you what happened Wednesday morning." Not waiting for Tom to answer, Clay stood up. "Bring your coffee and let's get comfortable in the living room. Before we get on the subject of Sid Duncan and the skunks he runs with, I want to fill you in on what Todd and his family have been doing. We got a letter from them just last week."

"I'm glad that partner of mine writes to someone," Tom said. "I haven't heard from him in a month of Sundays."

Tom Pickett had met Todd Fields Howard when Todd had arrived from San Francisco fourteen years ago. Todd had been nineteen then, and Tom twenty-three. They struck up an immediate friendship and, along with a riverboat captain by the name of Phillip Geyer, formed a partnership to run cattle to Central Oregon.

Todd's mother had died giving birth to her only child. She had been abandoned by Todd's father. After his mother's death, Todd had been taken in by his mother's best friend who later married Jamie Fields, a successful San Francisco merchant and land speculator. They had two daughters, Katy and Ann.

Todd's foster parents raised him as their own son, and loved him as much as if he were. It was in Oregon, on a cattle drive from the Willamette Valley to the Ochoco

Country that Todd and Tom first crossed paths with Clay and Ellie Howard. Later, Todd was to find out they were his maternal grandparents. Todd and Tom settled twenty miles due east of Prineville and became successful ranchers. Their investments in gold and shipping grew and prospered. In 1871 Todd left for San Francisco to marry the Field's daughter Ann, planning to return with his new bride. Three weeks after their marriage, Ann's father had a stroke. Todd stayed on to help run the family's many businesses. After the first year it became apparent Jamie Fields would not fully recover, so Todd stayed on. He now had two sons aged nine and eight, and a six-year old daughter, Mary, named after his mother. His first boy was named Jamie after the man who raised him, and his second son was christened Tom Pickett Howard, after Todd's partner and friend.

Once both men were settled in easy chairs, Clay pulled his reading glasses from his shirt pocket and carefully unfolded Todd's letter. He read its contents to Tom. It told how Todd's business holdings were growing as well as the latest news from San Francisco.

Clay grinned widely as he turned to the second page. "Todd says they went to see an English fellow named Oscar Wilde at the California Theater. Wilde talked about the nature of truth, beauty and what he called 'so forth.' He had to laugh at the man's attire. Listen to what he has to say: 'Wilde was dressed foppishly in a long velvet frock with pointed white shoes, yellow gloves and a puce colored tie. He wore a cream colored ten gallon hat, but certainly didn't look like any of the cowboys you'll find in Oregon! Although he is the rage here I'm afraid I found what he called his "discourse" to be very dull.' "

Clay chuckled as he continued. "But with Ann's sharp elbow, I managed to stay awake until it ended." There were two pages citing what the family had been doing, and Ann, Todd's wife, had added a note to tell them that Jamie Jr. had just gotten over a case of whooping cough and now his younger brother had come down with the measles.

At the end was a plea for Clay and Ellie to come visit them. When he finished, Clay put away his glasses, then laid the letter on a doilied end table by the chair. "Ellie and I sure would like to see Ann and Todd and our great grandchildren again," he voiced wistfully.

"Why don't you, Clay? You've got a good ramrod to watch your ranch. And I'll be around to lend a hand."

Clay glanced up, a preoccupied look in his eyes. He had scarcely heard Tom's offer.

"Tom, we're both needed here. I think this whole country is about to bust wide open. And it's going to be sooner than later, unless I miss my guess."

CHAPTER EIGHT

Tom searched his friend's face. In the time he had known Clay Howard, Tom had never seen him so upset.

"You think it's that bad?" he asked. Before he got his answer, he read it in the sorrowful look in Clay's eyes.

"It's worse than bad, Tom. You spend your time taking care of the ranch and minding your own business. That's the whole problem." He reached for his pipe on the table by his side and pulled a tobacco pouch out of his back pocket, stretching sideways to do so. "And that's what they're counting on."

Tom was puzzled. He wasn't sure what the gentle man was saying. He waited until Clay had filled and tamped the tobacco in place with his thumb, then lit his load. After exhaling several dense clouds of smoke, Clay continued.

"Most people mind their own affairs, but not Duncan and Cotter. They want to run the whole town. And probably will unless somebody stops them.

"Take the killings of Langdon and Harrison for instance. Our so-called vigilance group would like you to think Langdon was involved in rustling. Anyone with an ounce of sense knows that's not true."

"But why did they kill Harrison?" Tom exclaimed. "Reub Hassler says he saw him in town the day Crooks and Jory were killed, so he couldn't have been involved."

"That's my point," Clay raised his voice. "Everyone knows Harrison was in town that day. Duncan's bunch have become so arrogant that they killed him out of pure cussedness because he had made a remark about the local politicians who were throwing their weight around.

"I'll tell you something else," Clay leaned forward intently. "Langdon wasn't killed because of the murders either. He was shot because his land controls the pass between Shaniko and Crooked River."

Pickett's puzzled look prompted Clay to continue. "Sheep. The Duncan brothers and George Cotter want to keep sheep out of this part of the country. And Lucius Langdon wouldn't sell out to them." Clay Howard looked at his pipe, tamped it with his index finger and went on. "That's why they're so all-fired set on having a stockmen's protective association. Only you can just bet they won't ask anyone running sheep to join."

Shaniko, directly north of Prineville and halfway to The Dalles was gaining a reputation as a growing sheep town, as were the surrounding communities of Clarno, Fossil and Antelope. Cleek, another town that welcomed sheep was on the north side of Grizzly Mountain, located on the pass funnelling through Lucius Langdon's land.

"It's hard to believe they would kill two men over a few sheep," Tom said softly.

"Yes," Clay answered. "A few sheep and a need for power. Look at these facts." He touched the index finger of his left hand with the first finger of his right hand, bending the left finger back slightly. "One. Al Langdon, Lucius's brother, got a death note the day Lucius was shot and killed. It was signed with a skull and bones. Word is, he's leaving town. He told Lynn Wood, the barber, he'd rather be a live coward than a dead hero. Two," he touched his middle finger, "Lucius's wife Emma is selling out. And guess who the buyer is? None other than one of Sid Duncan's lackies. Three," he moved to the next finger, "John Ericksen, the Deputy Sheriff, wrote a letter to Sheriff Storrs at The Dalles to tell him that he felt the killings were justifiable and recommended the matter be

39

closed. And four," he repeatedly struck the small finger of his left hand, "Leo Fried got a skull and crossbones note threatening his life if he told what he saw.

"Look at some other facts too, Tom. Russell returned at two o'clock yesterday morning with Langdon and turned him over to Ericksen. Around four-thirty, eight men shot Lucius and dragged Harrison to the bridge where they hung him. Now, how do you suppose eight men got the word and were able to get organized in such a short period of time?

"And how about this? Duncan's bunch returned from Al Langdon's around midnight before the killings. Duncan and most of the men with him claimed they jumped ten rustlers. All of which escaped. Sound fishy to you? It did to me, too. I talked to Gil Wayne, who was with Duncan's posse. Wayne wouldn't go along with the story. Said a barking dog alerted one man who got away on a white horse. His guess was that it was Lucius, and he guessed right. According to Gil there was only one other man in the cabin, and that was Al."

Clay Howard slumped back into his chair and relit his pipe.

After a moment, Tom said, "Clay, if what you say is true, what's to be done?"

A heavy sigh escaped from Clay's lips. "Tom, I honestly don't know. I guess we had better stay alert, keep our eyes open, and try to find out if anyone else feels like I do."

"Feels like we do, Clay," Tom immediately responded. "You've convinced me."

After saying goodbye to Clay and Ellie, Tom guided his horse toward Main Street and Lynn Wood's Tonsorial Emporium, which was located next to the old Singer Saloon, now owned by Gil Wayne.

Even though he was deep in thought, he couldn't help but feel and see the excitement and bustle of a growing frontier town. Last summer there had only been three or four windmills providing the residents with water from their wells. Now there were dozens. And even more new homes stretched down the length of Deer and Beaver streets.

When he reached Main, Tom cantered past Fried and Hahns General Store, Kelley's Saloon and Maling's Planing Mill to a weathered door that faced two red and white striped poles which supported an overhanging balcony. Wrapping his reins around a lodgepole hitching rail, he tucked in his shirt, pulled up his pants and stepped inside. Wood nodded a greeting. On a stool that served as a barber's chair was Lester Simons, a homesteader from Powell Butte. Simons was a noted talker. He usually jumped from subject to subject so fast his listeners seldom knew which one he was talking about at any given time. Simons conversations were also one-sided, with Simons doing all of the talking. Such was the case now. He was expounding on the two years he spent in the Willamette Valley before he came to Central Oregon.

"1863. Can't remember a worse winter. Snow so high our old milk cow ate the moss off the trees I cut for firewood. Annie was her name. People didn't fare much better. 'Bout all there was to eat was dried beans, turnips and 'taters. I even knew a family that ate their cat. Bones and all."

Without pausing, Simons glanced out of the corner of his good left eye to see if Tom was listening. His other eye was white and unseeing from the cataract that covered it. "Remember old Doc Vanderpool who brought his medicine wagon here? The bright one, painted in red and yellow that was drug by two moth-eaten mules? My plowhorse was ailing so I bought some of his colic medicine. Did her a world of good. She was up off the ground after three spoonfuls. Cost me a dollar, but it was worth it. Never did

41

understand why he gave up medicine to become postmaster.

"Same year as the first school was built. On Mill Creek. 1868 wasn't it, Lynn?" Not giving the gaunt barber a chance to reply, he went on. "Yep, 1868. Teacher's name was Crawford. The only school between The Dalles and Klamath Falls. They had as many members of the school board as they did pupils. Never held to schoolin' myself. Figure if we need to count, that's why we have fingers and toes.

"Boiled wheat. Ate a lot of that in Brownsville. Seems..."

"There you are, Lester," Wood interrupted, taking an old bed sheet from around Simons's neck and giving it a good shake. "With the shave, that will be two-bits."

To keep Simons from starting up again, he turned to Pickett. "You're next, Tom. How are things at the 3C?"

Knowing the routine, Pickett picked up the conversation. Both men ignored Simons until he dug a quarter out of a cracked leather purse, and mumbling to himself, left.

Tom cranked a grin at the grey-haired barber. "I'm glad I'm not in your line of work. I'd hate to listen to that all day long."

"Oh, Lester's all right. Living by himself the way he does, I guess the only chance he gets to talk is when he comes to town. After you hear some of his stories a dozen times though, they do tend to get a mite old."

Tom and the barber made small talk as Wood pulled up his hair with a comb and began clipping. When Wood turned to put his scissors down and pick up a bottle of Rose Hair Tonic, Pickett swivelled on the stool to watch Wood's reaction to the question he was about to ask.

"Tell me, Lynn, what does everyone think of the killings?"

The hand that was reaching for the quart-sized bottle of red liquid froze. Then Wood picked it up, shook some of the pungent oily tonic in his other hand, rubbed his palms together and vigorously scrubbed it into Tom's scalp.

"Guess it makes a lot of people stop and ponder," he said cautiously.

"Clay Howard was telling me that Lucius's brother Al got a threatening note. Leo Fried, too. No signature, but a skull and crossbones on each one."

Tight-lipped, Lynn Wood replied, "Tom, I'm just a barber. And I want to live to be an old one. I hear a lot of things. I wouldn't say this to anyone but you, 'cause I know you won't pass it along. Folks are uneasy. There's been a lot of rustling lately. If these killings stop the thieving, then I guess the purpose has been served."

"Is that what you really think, Lynn?" Tom asked.

Wood's silence was his answer.

CHAPTER NINE

It was early November, eight months since the vigilantes shot Lucius Langdon and hung W. H. Harrison, his hired hand. Arne Swenson, the cook for the Columbia Cattle Company, had just returned from Prineville with a load of supplies. As was his custom, he stopped first at the ranch house to leave the mail and latest copies of *The Dalles Mountaineer* and Prineville's *Ochoco Pioneer* with Tom Pickett.

Tom was waiting on the steps of the plank building that served as his office and living quarters when Swenson pulled up.

"Anything going on in town, Arne?" Tom asked the genial gap-toothed cook.

"Nope. Price of eggs has gone up to fifty cents a dozen now," he said disgustedly. "Them hens is makin' more money than the miners on Scissors Creek." He started to pull away, then jerked his team to a stop. "Almost forgot," he said, pulling a folded letter from his shirt pocket and handing it to Pickett. "Clay Howard asked me to give you this." With a flick of the reins he turned toward the cookhouse to unload.

The summer had passed without incident, but Tom had made it a point to go to town at least once a month to check with Clay. He had been in Prineville only two weeks ago.

Pausing at the top step to open the envelope Swenson had given him, Tom pulled out the single sheet that was inside.

Tom:

> *There's something going on, but I can't put
> my finger on it. Duncan and Cotter are step-
> ping up their efforts to organize the cattlemen.
> They came to see me twice last week. The
> second time they had four more names added
> to their list. I wouldn't say their manner was
> exactly threatening, but it was close to it.*

Tom glanced up from the letter and stared vacantly at
the distant snowcapped peak of Lookout Mountain. His
lips pursed in thought. Tom mentioned to Clay during
their last visit that a group of cattlemen had ridden from
the Maury Mountains to urge him to join a cattle association that was being formed. The rustling of horses and
cattle had not stopped, and Tom was hearing more and
more complaints from ranchers located around Mitchell
and the north fork of Crooked River. He was missing two
mares himself, but wasn't sure whether they were taken
by rustlers or a wild stallion had run them off.

Looking back at the letter, he continued reading:

> *I don't know if you've seen Friday's Ochoco
> Pioneer yet. It mentions Governor Moody's ap-
> pointments for Crook County. Sid Duncan
> and his brother C. E. were in Salem for a
> month prior to this announcement, so I guess
> this is the result of their visit.*

> *Cotter and Duncan now have the power to
> control the county. Only time will tell if they
> use it wisely or for their own ends. If anything
> urgent develops that I think you should know
> about I'll send a rider.*

> *Clay*

Tom replaced the letter in the envelope and entered his office. He sat at his desk and picked up the latest copy of the *Ochoco Pioneer*. The large, bold headline jumped out at him: *CROOK COUNTY BILL PASSES. PRINEVILLE NAMED COUNTY SEAT.* Beneath the headline, a subhead read: *Battle with Senator Mitchell Over.*

He quickly scanned the story that followed, which told how the bill was introduced by B. F. Nichols, a Powell Butte rancher who represented Wasco County. The bill had been opposed by Senator John Mitchell, who through his influence as president of the Senate, had tabled it in the hope the town of Mitchell, which was named for him, would become the county seat. Through pressure by the House of Representatives, the Senate was forced to vote and passed the resolution that adopted the name of Crook, after Major General George Crook, Civil War hero and Indian fighter who had ended the Bannock uprising in Wasco county.

Tom glanced next at the article in the lower right-hand corner of the paper. It was headlined: *Republican Governor Appoints Democrats as Officers for New County.* Among those listed were Charles E. Duncan, county judge; Benjamin F. Alben, county commissioner; S. T. Richards, county clerk, and Gus Brinkley, treasurer. Norman Frazier was named as sheriff. This surprised Tom. Why not Ericksen, he asked himself. Or Bernhart?

The article concluded with a statement from the governor saying the appointments would be valid for two years. A general election for those officials would be held in June, 1884.

A cold chill ran down Tom's spine. Two years! More than enough time for Major Duncan and George Cotter to gain control of the new county. He picked up the most recent issue of *The Dalles Mountaineer*, which told a similar story. It listed the same appointees—with one exception. There would also be a sheep inspector who would report directly to the appointed officers of the new county.

There was an air of jubilation among the men gathered in the back room of the Wayne Saloon. Major Sid Duncan stood behind a felt-covered table usually used for poker. His posture was ramrod straight. Both hands were clasped behind his back. His eyes glistened with excitement. Had Clay Howard been there, he would have described him as puffed-up as a prairie hen. But Howard wasn't there. The people in the room were the new county appointees plus George Cotter, Charley Conwell, ex-Deputy Sheriff Ericksen and ex-Deputy Marshal Bernhart.

With a deliberate look at each of the occupants, who were seated around two other tables, Duncan began. "There are a number of things we need to discuss."

He told his audience in the smoky, low-ceilinged room how his eloquence had persuaded the state's new Republican governor to appoint the current slate of officers for Crook County. He did not add that the man really responsible for their selection was W. W. Thayer, the outgoing governor, a Democrat. A deal had been struck between Thayer and his Republican successor to reappoint certain of Thayer's political cronies in return for support of legislation Moody felt was vital to his administration.

"So," Duncan gloated. "One of our aims has been achieved. We have maintained our political status. Even improved it. And our second goal, that of organizing a cattle association, is all but wrapped up. We have enough names to make it a fact. George," he waved a hand in George Cotter's direction, "is drawing up the Association Constitution and By-laws now. He feels they'll be ready in

47

a few days." Reluctant to give up his position as center of attention he nevertheless turned to Cotter. "George, would you like to add a few words?"

Rising to his feet, Cotter took a step back. His hands gripped the chair he had been seated in. "First, let me congratulate the new county officers," he said.

His statement was followed by a burst of raucous laughter and a great deal of back slapping. "And let me also extend my congratulations to our new sheriff, Norman Frazier." Cotter put on a mock frown and directed his gaze at the former deputy sheriff. "John, the new governor felt you were neglect in your duties in that you should have resisted the mob that overpowered you and killed your prisoners. He couldn't go along with appointing you sheriff again."

The room exploded in laughter as those near Ericksen's table rose to gibe and jostle him.

George looked solemnly at Bernhart. "And, W. C., the formation of a new county just plumb eliminated your job. It looks like you'll have to put in a full day's work at blacksmithing."

For a brief moment something flickered in the eyes of W. C. Bernhart. Something reptilian, dark and evil. Then he smiled thinly and rose. "Either that, or maybe I can find a more profitable way to fill my time."

Raising both hands to still the voices of a group that had been working too long on the saloon's supply of rye, Cotter asked for quiet.

"There's work to be done. By all of us. The new By-laws are going to state that anyone who runs stock of any kind has to have a permit."

"What about sheep," a voice called out.

Looking at Charley Conwell, who posed the question, Cotter answered. "Sheep are stock. Anyone that wants a permit has to come to us. Besides," he added slyly, "that's why the constitution will carry the title of Cattlemen's Protective Association."

Major Sid Duncan jumped up, eager to again be in control of the meeting. "Thank you, George. There are some things that need to be said. One is that we have been appointed, not elected, so this presents a problem in that we report to the governor. Charles Cartwright, who lives in Shaniko, has also been appointed as county sheep inspector, but he reports to us. That means as far as sheep are concerned we tell the governor only what we want him to hear.

"Another thing to consider is that not everyone wants to join the Association. Howard, Pickett, Russell, Combs, Schwartz and Staats to name a few. Nor do most of the smaller cattlemen." White saliva formed at the corner of his mouth, and his steely blue eyes glinted, cold as morning frost. "Pickett, Russell and Howard we won't mess with yet. But that won't stop us from putting the squeeze on the others."

CHAPTER TEN

Bill Russell was hopping mad. For the second time, he read the notice posted in the window of the *Ochoco Pioneer.* Bold letters proclaimed: *Important Notice!!!* Then in smaller type below: *By order and decree of the newly formed Ochoco Cattlemen's Protective Association, a permit is required to move any stock on the following grazing lands: The Ochocos, Maury Mountains, Grizzly Peak and Crooked River Valley. Permits may be obtained from George Cotter at his office on Main Street.* The proclamation was signed by Major Sidney Duncan.

Russell spat out a curse and, with fire in his eyes, marched down the rutted dirt street to Heisler's General Dry Goods store. Heisler was standing on a ladder putting canned goods on an upper shelf when Russell burst in, his face was red as his brick-red hair.

Before Heisler could say a word, Russell's Irish temper lashed out. He shouted at the shirt-sleeved storekeeper. "I was born and raised in Oregon, and came to this part of the country when no more than a handful of people were here. I'll be damned if anyone is going to tell me where I can run my cattle. Particularly Cotter and his lackeys."

Heisler was wise enough to say nothing as Russell marched to the pine counter and continued his tirade. "Maybe they can buffalo other folks, but they better not mess with me. What handguns do you have in stock?"

"Two .41 Colts and three .32 Smith and Wessons, Bill," Heisler replied cautiously.

"I'll take 'em all. And 100 cartridges to go with each," Russell demanded. "And I'll take them right now. Anyone asks one of my riders for a permit and they'll get a hide full of lead instead."

Russell gathered up the guns and ammunition the store keeper had placed in a gunny sack, scrawled his name on a charge slip, and stormed out. William Heisler exhaled loudly, his breath ended in a whistle. "Guess he must have read the Cattlemen's notice. There's one man who will do just as he says," he mumbled to himself as he resumed stocking the shelves.

The notice about a horse race that was posted below the Cattlemen's Association flyer had escaped Russell's attention. Had he gone to the Wayne Saloon, that's all he would have heard. Ever since Barney Prine had established his combination saloon, store and blacksmith shop in 1868, foot and horse racing had become popular Prineville sports. When Prine became too old to run against all comers, he turned his energies to buying, selling and trading race horses. Most races were held during the summer months, but a local boy, Charles Luster, had a deep-chested bay that he had been training and in October issued a challenge to the owner of a spotted Indian pony named Kaleetan that had beaten all other horses it ran against.

The owner scoffed when Luster continued to challenge him. On Thanksgiving day, in Kelley's saloon, Luster braced him again. "I'll wager sixty dollars my horse can beat yours. Anytime, anywhere." Tom Congleton, the owner of the spotted pony had just finished two glasses of rye, and, goaded by his well-lubricated friends, accepted the offer on the spot. The race was set for Saturday, December 15th, when most of the area's residents would be in town for a Grange meeting.

It was now the eighth of December. Moe Cotter, George Cotter's younger brother, Charley Conwell and Bill Bernhart, the ex-Deputy Marshal, were sitting at a corner table in Gil Wayne's saloon trying to decide which horse they would bet on. Moe, who had turned seventeen two months ago, sneered at Conwell's suggestion the Warm Springs Indian pony would take the race. "Not in a thousand years. I've seen Luster racing that long-legged bay of his. He doesn't use a saddle, either. Nothin' can catch him."

Bernhart, still covered with charcoal grime from a day at the forge, drained his schooner of beer and wiped the foam from his lips with the sleeve of his work-stained canvas shirt. "From the betting that's going on, most everybody seems to agree with you. It's hard to find someone who will bet on the pony. He's good for a half-mile, but he's liable to run out of wind in this two-miler."

Conwell's close-set eyes became slits, and he leaned forward conspiratorially. With a nod of his head he indicated he wanted them closer. They hunched over the table. "Bill," he said. "You just gave me an idea. Let's put our money on the Indian nag, then go look up Luster. I know he's in town today. I saw him at the barber shop not more than an hour ago. Heard him say that after his bath there he was going to have supper then spend the night at the hotel."

"What's that got to do with the race?" Moe asked. He was physically strong and muscular for his age, but his mind had ceased to grow long before his body had. People had quit calling him simple-minded behind his back only because they had to answer to his older brother, George.

Conwell patiently explained. "Because we're going to pay him a visit and convince him he should throw the race."

52

Light dawned on Moe's face, which split into a wide grin. He rose with the others and they began circling the room placing their bets on the pony Kaleetan.

At Sam Jackson's Culver Hotel, Charlie Luster was having supper with his saddle partner and closest friend Sid Huston. They had been working part-time for Al Schwartz, a small rancher who ran sixty head of Durhams a few miles north of Prineville off the McKay Creek road. Schwartz was the one who had challenged Major Duncan's statement that the two peace officers guarding Lucius Langdon hadn't seen the killers.

Both youths were the same age as Moe Cotter, but, unlike Moe, were thin and slight. They were excitedly discussing the race.

"I think old Dan will beat Congleton's gelding by three or four lengths," Luster was telling his friend and companion. "I just wish I had more than sixty dollars to wager."

"Well, I still got forty dollars from our three month's work for Pa," Sid Huston replied. "Now all's I have to do is find a taker."

"You've got one," a cold voice directly behind him said. The two boys' heads jerked up from their meal. It was Charley Conwell. "Want to shake on it?" he asked.

Frightened by Conwell's unexpected appearance, as well as his reputation, Huston started to rise. His knees trembled so badly he sat back down. To hide their shaking he swivelled to face Conwell and crossed his legs. With what courage he could muster he said, "Sure," in a cracked whisper. Then he found his voice and replied in a more confident manner. "Forty dollars on Charlie's horse Dan. To win." He stuck out his hand to seal the deal.

It was all Huston could do to keep from crying out as Conwell squeezed his hand in a vice-like grip, applying even more pressure when he saw the pain it was causing the youngster.

"Now that the bet's settled, I need to have a word with your friend," Conwell said. "Alone." His cold eyes turned to Charlie Luster. "Outside, where it's private."

Without waiting for a reply he turned and walked out the rear door that led to the alley behind the hotel.

Luster licked his dry lips nervously and looked at his partner.

"What do you expect he wants to see me for, Sid?"

Huston's stomach turned sour as he faced his bunk mate. Beads of sweat formed on his forehead. "I don't know, Charlie, but I hope it's not what I think it is."

Partially paralyzed with fear, Luster rose clumsily, stumbling against the table.

"Want me to go with you?" Sid Huston asked.

"No. He said alone, and I don't doubt that's what he meant."

As Charlie Luster stepped into the dark alley he was immediately grabbed by two men and dragged into the shed where the hotel's supply of firewood was stacked. Before he could utter a sound, a beefy hand gripped his throat, choking off his voice. He was bodily lifted up in the air and slammed hard against the wall.

The grip eased and his feet touched ground. He spread his legs to hold himself up and gasped for air, holding his aching throat with his right hand.

"Now listen, and listen real good," a muffled voice whispered in his ear. "My two friends and me bet on the horse you're running against. And we don't intend to lose." The steel fingers tightened around Luster's throat once again as the speaker continued. "Understand?"

The whisper came again, before Luster could reply. "To show there's no hard feelings, we'll pay you back the sixty dollars you'll lose to Congleton." Three twenty dollar gold pieces were slipped into the front pocket of his rough wool shirt. The hand dropped from his neck.

Luster fought for breath, his lungs rasping in the night air. "I can't. . .," he started to say. A hard punch hit him low in the belly. He fell to his knees, retching and gasping, then his head was roughly jerked back by the hair.

"We ain't interested in no 'I can'ts.' We're just interested in seein' that you lose the race." Luster was hauled to his feet and kneed in the groin. As he dropped to the ground once more, one of the three shadowy figures stepped forward and kicked him hard in the ribs with heavy pointed range boots.

The kitchen door opened and threw its light on the three men. They jumped back, but not before Luster could identify who they were. A voice shouted out, "What's going on out there?"

"None of your business. Shut the door or I'll shut it for you."

The door was hastily closed.

One of the figures bent and hauled Luster up by the front of his shirt, his breath hot and sour on the boy's face. "Just so there's no misunderstanding, let's hear you say whose horse is going to win the race."

Seconds passed. When Luster didn't speak a sharp knife was pressed to his throat. "Think hard. If you give the wrong answer, you'll end your career as a jockey here and now, pumping your blood on the ground." The point was pressed against the skin, even harder, until all slack stopped.

"Congleton's." Luster sobbed, "Congleton's horse will win."

CHAPTER ELEVEN

The day of the race was unusually warm for mid-December. The temperature hung in the low 50's. It had been a mild winter, with only occasional light snow. The course was marked with stakes that flew red ribbons. It started in front of Prineville's first brick building and ran north on Main, through Ochoco Creek, up the hill past the cemetery, and on to the flats a mile away. There the riders were to circle a whitewashed barrel then follow the same route back. Judges were stationed by the barrel and at quarter-mile intervals to see that no shortcuts were taken.

To keep the horses from slipping, ashes from more than a hundred wood stoves and fireplaces had been collected and spread on the shaded patches of ice that spotted the ground.

Almost two hundred people had gathered to watch the contest. Behind the throng of adults, children played catch-me-if-you-can, chasing each other excitedly, their shrieks of laughter piercing the air. The girls were dressed warmly in linsey woolsey dresses with heavy stockings, and the boys, for the most part, wore buckskin pants and hickory shirts.

Miners from the Scissorsville and Mayflower mines came in on the Mitchell stage, not wanting to miss the fun. A number of Indian bucks had arrived from the Warm Springs reservation. Their expressionless faces contrasted sharply with the boisterous crowd that milled around them.

Ironically, the one man who had started the cow town's love for horse racing was not present. That was Barney Prine. A restless individual, he left in the early seventies to become City Marshal of Weston in northeastern Oregon. A brightly painted red, yellow and green medicine wagon had positioned itself in front of Brinkley's Dry Goods store. "Dr." Larkin Vanderpool had driven his two mules through the night from Shaniko to sell his famous Hostetters Stomach Bitters, a remedy for coughs, croup, asthma, bronchitis and that "tired and run down feeling." He was doing a brisk business and had to put a Closed For 20 Minutes sign on the side of his enclosed wagon while he refilled more bottles from the large barrel of whiskey and smaller barrel of molasses he kept inside. The concoction was eighty percent whiskey, twenty percent molasses, a touch of laudanum and a sprinkle of chittum bark. If he was chewing at the time, it also included a spit or two of tobacco.

People were still betting and Charley Conwell, Moe Cotter and Bill Bernhart, along with a select few they had let in on their secret, scurried from saloon to saloon placing their money on Congleton's horse.

The saloons were bursting with activity. Duncan, George Cotter and their cronies were lined up at the bar in Gil Wayne's saloon. Bill Russell and his friends were at Kelley's, and those 3C riders who could make it to town were having their drinks at Burmeister's or Graham's.

The race was scheduled for 1:00 p.m. Charlie Luster and Sid Huston had ridden into town earlier that morning and were in the livery stable. Both were slumped in the stall that held Luster's horse, Dan. Luster had barely slept all week. His throat was still raspy from the choking he got the week before and the skin over the ribs where he had been kicked was an ugly yellow and black.

"Sid, I just can't do it," he said to his companion. "It ain't right. Besides, you'll be out the forty dollars you bet Charley Conwell." He had tried to give Huston forty of the sixty dollars that had been slipped into his pocket, but Sid had refused to take it. He gave no reason, just tightened his lips and shook his head.

"Charlie, you got to lose, like it or not. That's one bunch you don't mess with."

Sick at heart, Luster rose and pulled his old cracked leather halter and bit over Dan's head. Taking the worn reins in his right hand, he led his saddleless horse out of the stable.

Kaleetan was already proudly prancing behind the starting line. As both riders mounted, a spontaneous cheer went up from the crowd.

Luster glanced up and spotted Charley Conwell. Conwell had his skinning knife out and was cleaning his nails. When he saw Charlie looking at him he grinned wickedly and put the blade to his throat and made a slicing motion.

The gun sounded and they sped off. Dan, in good spirits, immediately took the lead. As they passed the false front building that housed the newspaper he was a good length ahead. He gained even more ground on the hill leading to the cemetery and, ears flattened back, lengthened his stride on the flats. As he rounded the barrel that marked the half-way point, Luster saw Kaleetan lagging a good twenty yards behind.

Tears welled in Luster's eyes. "Damnit, Dan, you deserve to win," and without thinking spurred his horse. The gelding responded with even more speed. As they reached the dip before the cemetery, out of sight of the crowd and judges, Charlie Luster realized what he was doing. Sobbing, he jerked back hard on the reins. The confused horse slowed until his rider could see Congleton's pony closing on them.

The crowd at the finish line came into sight as they raced out of the dip, neck and neck. In the next few seconds Kaleetan surged ahead.

Dan, not knowing he was supposed to lose, saw the pony pass and strained against the leash. Charlie's arm ached as he tried to hold him back. They were less than a hundred yards from the finish line, with Congleton's horse two lengths ahead, when the worn reins snapped. It took the horse a fraction of a second to realize that he was no longer being restrained, and his rump lowered as he dug in his hind feet and shot ahead. All thought of winning or losing the race went out of Charlie Luster's mind as he fought to keep from falling by hanging on to the horse's neck. He could hear Dan's labored breathing, then lost his hold and tumbled to the ground.

He lay where he had fallen on the hard earth, too stunned to move. A roar filled his ears. The next thing he knew he was being lifted high in the air. Strong arms were supporting him. His mind cleared enough to realize the noise came from the throats of the excited crowd and that he was straddling the back of a giant miner who was holding him firmly by the legs. His throat tightened and became so dry he couldn't swallow. He groaned aloud as he realized that in spite of his efforts to hold Dan back he had won.

CHAPTER TWELVE

On the day following the race, Sunday, the saloons were packed and noisy. Most out-of-towners had spent the night in one of the two hotels, with friends or at the livery stable. Those who hadn't collected or paid their debts were doing so now. The finish of the race was told and retold dozens of times.

"Best race I ever saw, Bill," Sam Smith was saying to Bill Russell and John Combs, in Graham's saloon. " The best part of all was seeing Charley Conwell and his crowd on the short end of the stick."

"For sure, they didn't seem too happy about losing," Combs, a homesteader from the flats east of Prineville, chuckled.

As they talked, they were joined by a stout, short man who ran a small spread at Powell Butte, ten miles west of town. "They're not jumping up and down for joy, that's for sure," the new arrival, Steve Staats, added. He held up a fistful of bills. "The drinks are on me. Getting this fifty dollars from ol' W. C. Bernhart was like getting blood from a turnip."

As they elbowed their way to the bar, Smith posed a question. "Where's the Luster boy? You'd think he'd be celebrating with the rest of us winners."

Staats caught the bartender's eye, held up four fingers, and turned to his companions. "Frank Mogan told me he saw him and his buddy Huston light out right after the race. Maybe that fall shook him up worse than we all thought." As the brimming shots of whiskey arrived,

Staats picked his up. "Anyway, let's drink to him. It took a damn good horseman to win with a broken rein. Particularly one who finished half off his horse," he said, laughing.

Down the street, in a corner of the Wayne Saloon, George Cotter was having a heated argument with his younger brother and W. C. Bernhart. He was using the same argument he had given Charley Conwell an hour earlier.

"Don't be fools," his voice lashed at them. "Kill Luster tonight and everyone in town will know who did it and why. Use your heads. Give it a couple of weeks, then rig up a story about how you caught them with some stolen beef."

A loud shout interrupted their discussion. The babble of voices dwindled to silence as all attention focused on two men facing each other in front of the bar. The semicircle around them widened as those who had been close to the two backed away.

One of the men was Charley Conwell. Anger flashed from his dark eyes. His jaws clenched as he shifted position to face his bear-like opponent. Conwell spread his feet, slowly placed his glass on the counter, then returned his arm to his side where it held steady, inches from the butt of his gun.

The second man, mean-faced and surly, with several days growth of whiskers, stood his ground. He looked as if he'd been sleeping in a barn, and indeed he had. He paid a local farmer two bits a night for the three days he slept in the hay attic. It had been months since his clothes had seen water. The top two buttons of his wool shirt were missing, showing his grey-flannel underwear which was heavily crusted with dirt and mud and permanently stained by tobacco juice.

His name was Hank Vaughan. He had arrived in Prineville two years ago. Most of his time was spent

61

gambling and drinking. Occasionally, he did some riding for Bill Russell. He was a loner and a man to be left alone. Vaughan's past was well-known in Prineville. He and a partner had stolen a horse in Umatilla and fled across the mountains to Burnt River where they were surprised by Sheriff Frank Maddock and his deputy. In the gun battle that followed, Vaughan's companion and the deputy were killed. Vaughan surrendered, but not before he put a bullet through the sheriff's mouth—taking several teeth with it.

Vaughan spent ten years in prison. After he was released he married an Indian woman, the widow of an Army officer who had died and left her a good deal of inherited money. Vaughan's marriage lasted just long enough for him to get his hands on most of the money. When he did, he left Umatilla for the Washington Territory. He passed through Weston where he had a run-in with Barney Prine. After this he kept on the move from Walla Walla to Canyon City and eventually ended up in Prineville.

Vaughan's voice, slurred by too much liquor, broke the silence. "What I said, Charley, was that you're a chicken-livered, low-down welcher. I bet you two gold eagles that Luster would win and now you're trying to back out. You got two choices. Either pay up or go for your hogleg."

Conwell stared hard and long at his opponent. Had Vaughan been sober, he would have been able to catch the flicker in Conwell's eyes before Conwell drew. But Vaughan was a long way from being sober. Conwell's first shot creased Vaughan's forehead and the second entered his left breast, breaking a rib as it passed through his body. The impact of the bullet spun Vaughan around and sent him to the floor.

Sure that his shot had entered Vaughan's heart, Conwell stepped forward, his gun hand lax at his side. As he put his toe under Vaughan's stomach to turn him over,

Vaughan rolled onto his left elbow, yelled "damn yore eyes" and fired three times. Each of the shots hit Conwell in and below the left shoulder, shattering his shoulder blade and driving him against the bar, where he tried to brace himself. The shock of the heavy caliber bullets was too much. His gun dropped from a hand that had gone numb. As it clattered to the floor, he slid slowly down the plank front of the bar, his legs spread wide. Blood pumped in bright red spurts from three dark-rimmed holes in Conwell's shirt.

The silence that followed was shattered by the tolling of the single bell in the Union Church as it called its parishioners to Sunday service. Its last lingering ring paralyzed every man in the room until Gil Wayne called out, "Someone fetch Doc McClure before they both bleed to death." McClure was the town dentist, but that didn't seem to bother anyone. He was the closest thing to a doctor Prineville had.

McClure arrived, carrying a cracked medical bag. He bent to examine Charley Conwell, mainly because Conwell was the first body he came to. After stuffing several wads of cotton in Conwell's wounds he looked up. "Carry him to my office, I'll work on him there." Then he hurried to Hank Vaughan. He lifted an eyelid and saw nothing but white. Next he examined the furrow on the unconscious man's head and pulled up a flap of scalp to see if the bullet had entered the skull. Sucking his teeth, a habit he had when engrossed in his work, McClure tore loose Vaughan's filthy shirt and underwear to examine the chest wound. The blood was crusted and black, with just a trace of bright red seepage.

"Better haul him over to Dick Graham's. He might as well die where he's going to be boxed as here."

It took four stout miners to carry the giant to Graham's back door, where the undertaking work was done. Graham arrived, still wearing his bartender's apron, and instructed them to put Vaughan on the table. As he was bending over to look at the wounds, Bill Russell and Sam Smith entered from the rear door.

"Heard Hank was in here," Russell's deep voice boomed out.

At the mention of his name, Vaughan stirred. "That you, Bill?" he whispered weakly.

Russell moved to the table. "It is, Hank." Reaching up to touch Russell on the arm, Vaughan motioned him down. Russell stooped to put his ear next to Vaughan's lips.

"Bill, do me a favor. My Daddy said I'd die with my boots on, so take em' off, would you?"

As he pulled at the scuffed and muddy saddle boots, Russell turned to Smith. " Find one of my riders. Tell him to fill a wagon with straw and drive it over here. If Hank's going to cash in I'd just as soon have him do it at my place than the rear end of a saloon."

Before he lost consciousness, a single rational thought flashed through Vaughan's mind. Is Russell doing this out of kindness to me or does he want to keep me at his house where I can't talk?

CHAPTER THIRTEEN

A raw wind blew out of the northwest, numbing Tom Pickett's face and misting his eyes with tears. The sun had just broken over the mountain range as he left the 3C ranch and turned west toward Prineville.

Frozen ice crystals hung suspended in the air, glittering like diamonds in the bright, clear light. The wind stirred drifts of new snow, making circular patterns on the frozen melt of the day before.

It was so cold no animals or birds were out; not even a scavenging hawk. Billows of steam from his horse's nostrils blurred Tom's vision as the spirited gelding eased its way down an ice-crusted slope to the trail by frozen Ochoco Creek. Winter had finally arrived. And with a vengeance.

Tom never tired of the trip to town. No matter what time of year it was, there was always something new to see. Or something different in what he had seen a dozen times before. The trip always gave him time for his own thoughts. It was the day before Christmas and he was looking forward to a visit with Ellie and Clay Howard. He had considered riding in on Christmas day, but the weather had been so unpredictable he decided to spend the night at the Culver Hotel in case a blizzard hit.

Tom's eyes drifted to the imposing sentinels of rimrock that lined his way. The complexity of ridges stood straight and tall, like soldiers on parade. His horse, accustomed to the route, needed no guidance. It automatically turned to the abrupt rise that would lead Tom to a point where the wind would be less severe and he would be level with the surrounding plateaus. As he topped the rise, majestic snow-peaked Mount Jefferson appeared. A quarter of a mile farther, four more mountains loomed on the horizon: the Three Sisters and Broken Top. They stood, clear and imposing, against a cloudless backdrop of pale blue sky.

"Looks like we might have nice weather tomorrow, Ted," he told his buckskin. Like most cowmen, he talked to his horse a good deal. As one old range rider observed, "It's nice being able to talk to your horse, 'cause you know they won't talk back and ask a lot of fool questions."

As he dropped lower into the valley, past Mill Creek, the freezing wind struck again. Tom paused to raise the collar of his sheepskin coat, then gently touched the flanks of his horse with his spurs to resume his journey. The bitter chill reminded him of the two hard winters that followed each other in '79 and '80. Then again in '80 and '81.

He and his partner, Todd Fields Howard, had arrived in this lush grass country in 1870. For nine years their herd had slowly grown and they had prospered. In the mid-seventies, beef prices were so high that many local ranchers had been bought out by eastern interests who saw a way of making a quick and substantial return on their investment. This bothered the town merchants who lost business because these outfits had no loyalty to Prineville and bought their supplies where they were located back east, or in San Francisco and Portland where they could get bigger discounts for their large purchases.

Probably the reason, Tom thought, that to this day most of the local merchants still seemed to favor the group that didn't have this advantage; the homesteaders and small ranchers.

Tom winced as he recalled the two consecutive winters that had almost wiped out the Columbia Cattle

Company. In those two hard seasons he and Todd lost eighty percent of their stock. Many ranches lost all of their animals. The first of these disastrous winters had been deceiving. The second one was pure agony.

Winter arrived late in 1879, and began as a mild one. Cattle and horses ranged in the lower pasture lands where forage was easy. In mid-February of 1880 a Chinook hit the area, melting what little snow there was in the mountains. The warm, moist southwest wind brought spring-like outings by homesteaders and ranchers that usually took place in May or June. The stock drifted to higher elevations where tempting new shoots of bunch grass grew from the recently warmed soil. Ranchers, confused by the weather, let them wander to fatten up.

Late February, without warning, an arctic front moved over the area. Overnight two feet of snow fell. Five days later, six feet of snow covered the ground.

Frantic stockmen, their horses floundering helplessly in the frozen drifts, tried to find their cattle.

They located a few by tracking blood that came from the feet of their stock which had been cut on the icy edges of rain-frozen snow. Most that were found were either dead or so near death they couldn't be coaxed to their feet.

At night, as the ranchers and their families huddled around glowing iron stoves, they could hear the wild cries of coyotes and wolves as they surrounded and attacked these helpless creatures.

The following winter of 1880 arrived earlier than usual, with snow and freezing winds. By December, temperatures ranged from 35 to 40 degrees below zero. Snow drifts as high as ten feet made it difficult, sometimes impossible, for ranchers to reach those cattle that had gathered around their outbuildings. Many dug tunnels in a frantic attempt to locate them. The snowpack held for ninety days, then melted rapidly. A week of unusually warm weather followed. Livestock that had somehow managed to escape the severe weather headed for the river banks where there was food. Many were caught in those lowland areas and drowned in floods that swept down the swollen streams.

Tom made a conscious effort to shake the painful memory from his mind. It's no wonder so many bankrupt cattlemen turned to rustling, he thought. They had to feed their families somehow. Before these two hellish winters the large ranches, smaller cattlemen and homesteaders were interdependent on one another. The smaller ranchmen and homesteaders worked for the large spreads to supplement their income. Their common enemy was hostile Indians. Each group was few in number, so no conflict for the land existed until a wave of settlers and cattlemen swarmed to the area.

"Things sure have changed some since we first came here, Ted," Tom said aloud, his thoughts becoming vocal. "Now most everyone seems to be looking out for himself, and the devil take the hindmost."

Rustling had become so bad after these two fierce winters that cowmen had taken to hiding their brands. One cagey rancher on Crooked River, Lyon Lawrence, was putting his mark between the toes of his cattle, and often could be seen on his hands and knees examining his neighbor's stock.

It was close to noon when Tom hit Monroe Street. The smell of coffee and salt pork filled the air as Prineville's residents prepared their noon meal. Ted, anticipating his usual reward of grain at Gil Wayne's new livery, picked up his pace.

Once his mount was seen to, Tom crossed the frozen street to the barbershop for a haircut and to catch up on the latest news. When he entered he found Lynn Wood dozing in one of the cane waiting chairs. "Business slow, Lynn?" Tom called out, waking the barber.

"Yep, 'tis. Most people had their ears lowered the weekend of the race," Wood said groggily, getting slowly to his feet. "Have a seat."

"I wasn't in when Luster won. Hear it was quite a show," Tom stated.

"More than a show it seems. Al Schwartz came to town this morning, mad as a wet hen. Said the Huston boy told him Luster was supposed to lose but his horse had other ideas. Seems Conwell, Bernhart and young Moe Cotter worked Luster over in an alley until Charlie agreed to throw the race. He was holding that bay of his back until his reins snapped."

Tom stiffened. "That's a pretty strong accusation."

"Too strong if you ask me. What Schwartz is saying ain't going to sit well with those he's accusin'. Even if what he's saying is true he should keep his mouth shut."

Tom silently agreed, and changed the subject. "Anything else happening that's worth hearing about?"

Wood paused in his clipping, comb in one hand, shears in the other. "Yep. A couple of things. Old man Cotter has been named Justice of the Peace. I'd guess his son George had a hand in that." The slight barber stood back to look at his work, then resumed cutting and talking.

"A. J. Tethrow is going to put a ferry across the Deschutes. Where the county road crosses. Told me the license cost him twelve dollars and fifty cents. I imagine he'll make it back in a hurry, though. A. J. says he's going to charge a nickel for every sheep and hog, a dime for each horse or cow, and fifty cents for a wagon and team. Says he'll be one of the richest men in the county in a couple of years."

"I expect he'll have more invested than the license fee," Tom replied. "That Deschutes can get pretty mean in winter. Any ferry rigging he puts up will have to take the spring floods and uprooted trees the river will be carrying."

Holding up a cracked and stained mirror, Wood asked, "Short enough?"

At Tom's nod, the loquacious barber began another subject as he gave Tom's scalp a hard massage. "Guess you heard about the shootout between Charley Conwell and Hank Vaughan." Without waiting for a reply he added, "Looks like Vaughan's going to live. Bill Russell took care of him for awhile, but he's living at the stable now and talking about leaving for Washington. As for Conwell, I doubt he'll be bothering anyone else for while, seeing as to how he can't use his gun arm."

Wood shook out the towel he had placed around Tom's neck as the wiry cattleman stood up, stretched and pulled a quarter from his watch pocket. "Keep the change, Lynn."

As he stepped to the door, Wood called out. "I shouldn't be saying this, but I know the mood of this town. I like Al Schwartz. If you see him, you ought to tell him to keep a clamp on his mouth. He may be biting off more than he can chew by taking on Conwell, Bernhart and Cotter."

CHAPTER FOURTEEN

As Tom left the barbershop, he pulled up the collar of his coat and wheeled to put the wind to his back. His neck, now unprotected by collar length hair, stung from the cold and Lynn Wood's bay rum tonic.

The first order of the day had been a haircut. The second a hot meal. Then he would stop at Lou Senders' Mercantile to place an order for Arne Swenson, the 3C cook. Afterwards he would visit the blacksmith shop and order two new branding irons.

As Tom left the Antler Cafe for Senders' store his heart picked up a beat. He was hoping Mary Katherine Reed would be there, yet he almost half-wished she wouldn't. If she were, he'd get all tongue-tied and act like a darned fool; not knowing what to say, and when he did say something it was usually the wrong thing.

Mary Katherine had been staying with the childless Senders ever since her parents and older brother had been killed by a band of Snake Indians, led by Paulina. The incident happened shortly after they had burned Jim Clark's stage relay station in the John Day country. The Reeds were homesteading on Cherry Creek when Paulina passed by with Clark's remuda of horses. Although the Reeds had nothing he wanted, Paulina vented his hatred of the whites by killing their milk cow and burning their cabin while they watched. Afterwards he tortured and killed the three Reeds.

Mary Katherine, or Mary Kay as most folks called her, had not been at home when the savages struck. Her

71

brother had scarlet fever so she was sent to stay with the Clarno family.

Lou Senders and his wife Martha had been good friends of Mary Kay's parents. When they got word that the Reed's cabin had been burned, Lou hitched his team, loaded it with supplies, and raced north to see if he could be of help. He didn't know until he got there that the Reeds had been killed. A neighbor told him Mary Kay was staying with the Clarnos until other members of the Reed family could be located. Knowing that Mary Kay had no living relatives, Senders continued on to the Clarno ranch in Antelope Valley. Once there he left his supplies with Andy Clarno, who was happy to get them, and took Mary Kay back to Prineville with him. That was sixteen years ago. Mary Kay had been four at the time.

As Tom entered the store, a blast of warm air from the circular iron Cleveland stove greeted him. A spring bell over the door announced his presence.

Tom always enjoyed visiting Senders. The scents of spices, apples, dried fruit and molasses mixed pleasantly with the odor of new leather goods, canvas and oiled harness. They were comforting smells, reassuring him that everything was in its right place in the world.

Behind the counter, measuring a bolt of cloth, was a pretty, slim-waisted girl who was just entering the full bloom of womanhood. Her erect posture carried the impression of self-confidence, which was mirrored in her deep blue, almost violet, eyes. Soft auburn hair hung down her back and cascaded over her shoulders.

She looked up to see who had entered, and her face lit with pleasure. "Merry Christmas, Tom," she said, then hurried from behind the counter to greet him. The freshly shaven back of Tom's neck flushed a bright shade of red, as did his face. He removed his hat and shifted nervously. "Afternoon, Mary Kay."

"Good afternoon yourself, stranger. I was just thinking about you the other day." She, too, blushed, then lowered her head. "I was wondering if you would be in before Christmas."

"Guess so." Tom nodded, his throat suddenly gone dry. "Going to have dinner with the Howards."

"Such nice people. I see Mrs. Howard every now and then. She always tells me when she's seen you, and what you've been doing."

She tentatively reached out and touched Tom's arm lightly with her slender fingers. "I know it's early," she said shyly. "But I was wondering if you're going to the Grange dance this spring?"

Tom swallowed hard. "Well, I hadn't thought much about it. . ." He hadn't completed his sentence when he saw a hurt expression cross Mary Kay's delicate face.

She turned and marched behind the counter, head held high. The warmth in her voice was gone. "Well, the only reason I asked was because Karl Miller thought I might like to go with him. I didn't say yes, but I didn't say no either."

Tom's mouth dropped in surprise. "Dutch Miller of The Lost Pick mine? He's old enough to be your grandfather!"

Mary Kay's jaw set and her eyes flashed. "Karl may be several years older than you are, but he's a gentleman. And even though he lives at Howard, he finds time to come to town to visit once a month. That's a lot more often than you do." To make her point, Mary Kay added, "And Howard is ten miles farther away than your old 3C ranch."

Anger stood between them like a wall. Tom fumbled in his coat pocket and brought out a creased paper. He laid it on the counter. "Arne needs these supplies. I'll pick them up tomorrow."

"Tomorrow is Christmas and we're closed. You can pick them up tonight or the day after Christmas, as you wish." Her eyes filled with tears. "Now, if there's nothing else you need, I have work to do."

Tom slammed his hat on his head and stalked out. "What's she so put out about," he muttered to himself as the bell jingled his departure. "I only told her what was on my mind."

He paused at the stoop wondering whether to go back in, but not knowing what he would say if he did, he walked away. Bernhart's blacksmith shop was just down the street. He would place his order for the irons, then let the Howards know he was in town.

The acrid smell of the smithy bit into his nostrils as he stood before the barn-size doors that were covered with dozens of brands that had been burned into them. The forge was silent, and he could hear no one working hot iron. As he stepped from the bright day into the dim interior, Tom's eyes strained to adjust. He barely made out three shadowy figures huddled together at the rear of the building. When they saw him, two quickly left by the side door. But not before Tom's ears picked up the words, "I'll take care of the stove. You just see that he's seated with his back to the window, and that it's open."

The remaining man stepped forward. A slant of sunlight from one of the many cracks in the hand-sawn plank wall caught his face. Huge arms hung from muscled shoulders. It was W. C. Bernhart.

"Well, Pickett, what brings you to town?"

"Need some new branding irons, W. C.," Tom said. "No hurry. Just thought I would place the order as long as I'm in town." Referring to the two who had just left, he added, "Didn't mean to interrupt anything."

Bernhart gave him a sharp look, then smiled innocently.

"Nothing important. Just two homesteaders wanting a wagon wheel fixed. Be glad to bend a little iron for you. Same length as last time?"

"Same length's fine."

"Staying in town?" Bernhart asked, almost too casually.

"At the Culver."

"It's a long ride from your place. Imagine you'll hit the hay early."

Not sure what the leather-aproned blacksmith was hinting at, Tom replied, "I'm not much of a nighthawk, so I probably will."

Tom had just finished a lonely supper and was standing on the hotel's veranda watching the town shut down. Dusk had fallen and the flicker of coal oil lamps pinpointed the night. In sharp contrast, blazes of light from the town's four saloons lit up the sidewalks and the portion of Main Street they faced.

Two hours ago Tom had picked up his sack of supplies from Senders'. As he entered, he saw Mary Kay look up, then disappear into the back room. Lou Senders greeted him and they made small talk while the bill was checked and totaled. Tom went through the pretense of looking at saddles, dawdling in the hope Mary Kay would reappear. When it became apparent she wasn't going to, he nodded to the tall grey-haired storekeeper, who wished him a merry Christmas, and left.

Too restless to sleep, Tom stepped out into the street and headed for Burmeister's Saloon where bursts of laughter filled the night air. He shouldered aside the gate doors and stepped inside.

Standing at the center of the bar was Jerry Noble. Tom grinned. He had made the right choice of saloons. Noble was one of the funniest storytellers in town. The people around him were doubled over in laughter, wiping tears from their eyes.

Noble saw Tom enter, waved and called out, "You're just in time to hear about the preacher who visited Mill Creek school, Tom." The thought of another story brought shrieks of laughter from two trail hands who obviously had drunk more than their fair share of tanglefoot.

Encouraged by the reception he was getting, the short, sandy-haired butcher put on a mock-serious face. "Seems this travelin' preacher went to the school to rail against sin and scare the pants off the pupils about Hell and Damnation. He carried on so long that it got dark and teacher Birdsong had to stop him.

"Anyway," Noble paused to take a long swallow from his mug of beer, "while he was gabbin', some of the more lively students sneaked out the back door and put the saddle of his mule on backwards. At the close of his sermon the preacher said his amens and left. He grabbed the reins in the dark and after several unsuccessful attempts to mount yelled out a string of curses that made him sound more like a mule skinner than a bonafide man of the cloth.

"This blasphemy, coming from the mouth of a minister, broke the culprits up. Hearing their snickers, he grabbed the cane punishment whip he carried in his rifle boot and chased them down the road, swearing with each step. When he got back he found the mule had got tired of waiting for him and left." Tears of amusement swelled in Noble's green-flecked eyes. He rubbed them with the back of a hairy hand and finished, laughing at his own joke. "He ended up walking ten miles back to town!"

While the jolly butcher was talking, Tom noticed Al Schwartz enter the saloon and walk unsteadily to the bar. Gus Brinkley and Sam Richards flanked him, and were setting up the drinks. A short time later the three joined two miners who were playing cards. Tom watched as they dealt a hand of seven-up. He debated whether to wander over, but felt this wasn't an appropriate time to see Schwartz and pass along Lynn Wood's warning.

No one paid any attention to Cal Jones, one of Major Duncan's riders, as he carried in an armload of wood and approached the large pot-bellied stove. It was generally understood that if you were cold it was up to you to bring in the firewood.

Jones lifted the handle with the toe of his scuffed boot and pulled the ornate door open. Then he stuffed in several sticks of juniper. One piece had been dipped in tar. After closing the door of the stove, he turned and left. Soon afterwards a dense, choking smoke filled the room.

Richards coughed, swore and got up. Circling the table, he opened the window behind Schwartz, then announced he was going to the bar for another round of drinks.

The oily smoke stung Tom's eyes, and as he had finished his drink and Noble seemed to have exhausted his supply of tales, he saw no reason to stay. Before leaving he glanced at the poker table. Schwartz was closing the window Richards had just opened. He heard Schwartz say, "To hell with the smoke, it's too cold with the window open."

Tom was pushing open the doors to leave when he heard a shot. Spinning on his heels he crouched and drew his gun, looking for its source. His eyes followed those of the crowd in the smoke-filled room. They were all focused on the corner where, in a pool of bloody chips, cards and glass, Schwartz lay sprawled face down on the felt covered table. He had been shot in the back of the head through the closed window.

CHAPTER FIFTEEN

That night, Tom slept fitfully. The combination of a bed he wasn't used to and the killing of Schwartz had put him on edge.

When the first pale light of dawn eased through the chintz curtains of his room, he sat up, pulled on his pants and, out of habit, shook out his boots before putting them on. Slipping into his pullover wool shirt, he picked up the crockery basin that sat on the washstand and went downstairs to the kitchen for hot water. Back in his room, he splashed water on his face and rubbed it over the back of his neck and through his hair. This ritual completed, he lathered his cheeks with the bar of lye soap that had been left by the basin and shaved, peering hard at the yellowed mirror that hung over the stand.

When he had scraped his face clean, he bent over the bowl, filled both hands with water and washed off what soap was left. He dried his face, combed his hair with a broken-toothed comb that had been left by the basin, and went downstairs.

The dining area was full. He headed for the large table in the middle of the room where one seat was left. Dropping his hat on the floor, he sat down. The only concession the hotel had made to the holiday was a chalked 'Merry Xmas' on the slate near the door that listed the menu.

Tom knew all of the people at the table: Steve Staats from Powell Butte; Sam Smith, who had come from Brownsville with Bill Russell; John Combs, who ranched southeast of town, and Jeb Stuart, a partner in Stuart & Pett Grist Mill which was located on the bank of Crooked River at the west end of Second Street.

Tom glanced briefly at each one and nodded a greeting. Obviously, the topic of conversation was the shooting of the night before. They were all grim-faced and tight-lipped. Pickett knew these men opposed the Cattlemen's Association, as he did. And as had Al Schwartz, last night's victim.

Steve Staats, to his immediate right, turned toward Tom. "Guess you heard of the killings last night."

Tom started to reply that he had in fact witnessed it, when the full impact of what Staats said hit him.

"Killings? Did you say killings? I was in Burmeister's when Schwartz was shot. That's the only one I know about."

Combs glanced up from his plate. "A bunch of riders shot and hung Sid Huston and Charlie Luster early this morning. Bill Russell and Sam here," he pointed his fork at Smith, "found their bodies dangling from that big juniper by young Cotter's corral. Side by side. So full of holes it looked like they were used for target practice."

When Combs paused to swallow some coffee, Sam Smith picked up where Combs left off. "Last night, preacher Neese rode up McKay Road to tell Mrs. Schwartz about her husband being shot. As he didn't see Huston or Luster, he asked if they were around to help bring the body home. She said Moe Cotter had ridden by earlier. He wanted to show them some work that needed to be done at his place, and they went with him."

The four men who had been seated at the table before Tom arrived exchanged knowing glances as Smith went on. "That isn't all. When Bill and I found them this morning there was a skull and crossbones note in Luster's pocket saying 'This is what happens to cattle thieves.'"

79

Smith continued. "Cotter wasn't home, and we don't know where he is. After breakfast Bill Russell and the four of us are going to look for him. We intend to ask him a few questions. Want to come along?"

"I'd like to, but I promised Ellie and Clay I would be there for Christmas dinner and I don't want to disappoint them," Tom replied.

Smith nodded his understanding. "We stopped by to tell Clay before we came here. Should we find out anything, we'll stop by."

Tom unlatched the Howard's picket fence gate. Before he reached the house, he caught the smell of roast goose, one of Ellie's specialties. Tom felt a touch of envy when he thought of Clay's comfortable home and the special feeling he and Ellie had for each other. Running a ranch and male companionship had always been enough for Tom. Yet, in the last few years he felt as if something were missing, as if his life wasn't complete. Since his partner Todd left to get married and settle down in San Francisco, there was no one who he could really talk to or share his innermost feelings with. "Why," the thought came to him, "I'll be thirty-seven this year. And I called Dutch Miller an old man!"

Before he could knock, Clay opened the door. His usually genial face was tight and drawn. They gripped hands firmly.

"Merry Christmas, Tom," he said somberly.

Ellie hurried from the kitchen, her face flushed from cooking, to add her greetings. "You two sit and visit for a spell. Dinner won't be ready for awhile yet."

Clay led Tom into the front room. "Guess you heard the news?" Clay said as they settled in comfortably-worn leather chairs.

"I was at Burmeister's last night when Schwartz was shot. Met Sam Smith and some others having breakfast at the hotel this morning. They filled me in on Luster and Huston." Tom then told Clay about the snatches of conversation he had heard while at the blacksmith shop. "It's not good, Tom. Things are coming to a boil too fast. The Cattlemen's Association has turned into nothing but a front for a bunch of self-appointed vigilantes. First Langdon and Harrison, now Schwartz, Luster and Huston. Five men dead."

"Clay," Tom replied, "There's no doubt a lot of rustling is going on. We're all feeling it."

"That's just the point," Clay shot back. "Our so-called vigilance group is getting rid of those who disagree with them, yet nothing is being done to stop the rustling."

Clay leaned forward and pounded a knee with his work-hardened fist. "If this keeps up, those of us who don't give in to them won't be safe." He looked directly at Tom. "I've been talking to a few people. We think maybe it's time to check out the players."

Seeing Tom's puzzled expression, he explained, "It's time to find out who we can count on when the pinch comes and we need to know exactly who's on what side. Like that book Ellie's reading." He pointed at a leather bound book on a side table.

Tom rose, picked up the thin volume, read the title and glanced back at Clay. His frown deepened. "A Tale of Two Cities? By Dickens?"

"Yep," Clay leaned back and turned his head toward the kitchen. "Ellie, what's the name of that woman who was knitting names in a shawl?"

Ellie called back, "Madame Defarge."

"That's the one," Clay grunted, "and that's what I'm doing."

More puzzled than ever, Tom asked, "You're knitting names?"

"No, but like that french woman, I'm collecting them."
He rose and went to his roll-top desk. Pulling open the bottom drawer he withdrew a ledger with one hand and tapped it with the forefinger of his other. "Right here."

He opened it and handed it to Tom. One page was headed "Vigilantes," the other, with a question mark. The names under Vigilantes started with Major Sid Duncan and was followed by George Cotter. Below Cotter's name a number of prominent citizens and ranchers were listed.

Tom glanced up. "Why a question mark on the second page?"

"Because I don't know what to call us yet."

Under the question mark was an equally long list of names. Tom's followed Clay's, which was first. Others were :

Sam Smith

John Combs

Al Schwartz

Steve Staats

Jeb Stuart

Claude Pett

Clay Neese

The Mogan boys (Mike and Frank)

David Stewart

David Templeton

Al Lyle

Isaac Ketchum

F. H. McDonald

As Tom finished Clay said, "As you can see, we're now one short." He was referring to Al Schwartz.

Tom sat back, thinking. Then he spoke. "Clay, you're missing a name. Bill Russell."

"Thought you might have noticed that. Turn the page."

The third page was titled "Not Sure." It contained two names: Bill Russell and Gilbert Wayne.

Tom started to ask a question, but just then Ellie came into the room, pulling off her apron. "Dinner's on the table. Tom, I hope you brought a big appetite with you."

They had just finished Ellie's bountiful meal and were returning to the living room to relax when three riders pulled up in front of the house. Clay pulled back the lace curtains and glanced out. "It's Smith, Staats and Russell." He hurried to the door, opened it, and called out. "Come on in, fellers. You're just in time for a piece of pie and cup of coffee."

"It would be mighty welcome," Staats said as they tramped into the house. "We haven't had a bite since breakfast."

Ellie, who had heard them arrive and also heard Clay's offer and Staats reply, said, "Sakes alive. There's plenty more than just pie and coffee. Come in the kitchen and fix a plate."

The three men eagerly complied. As they wolfed down their Christmas meal, Clay and Tom pulled up two sidechairs.

"It's about what you'd expect, Clay," Staats said, shoveling a last forkful of mashed potatoes into his mouth. "We found Moe back at his place. Says he spent the night with his brother George, who swears Moe was there." He reached for a hot biscuit. "Moe said Mrs.

Schwartz must be confused. Claims he was on his way to town when he met Sid and Charlie who were riding out to fix some fence. Says he left them where McKay Road heads toward Grizzly."

Russell cut in. "When we asked him why the two boys were found at his place his answer was 'Your guess is as good as mine.' He reckoned they'd been caught by the Association's vigilance group trying to steal some cattle he had in his corral."

Russell paused, helped himself to more cranberries, and continued.

"Two other things we learned. One is, we found Luster's gun in Cotter's yard. There were two spent cartridges in it, so he must have got off a couple of rounds before they nailed him. When Dick Graham examined the bodies he said he thought the boys were shot then hung, and while they were hanging were riddled with bullets. Dick says he could tell this because they didn't bleed from all the bullet holes.

"The other thing we found out is that Bernhart is in his shack being guarded by Duncan and John Ericksen. They say he was kicked in the head by a horse he was shoeing early this morning. They won't let anybody see him. Not even Doc McClure."

Pushing aside his plate, Russell added, "The three of us figure maybe Luster shot one of them before they got him, and it just might have been Bernhart."

CHAPTER SIXTEEN

Three days after the murders of Schwartz, Huston and Luster, the *Ochoco Pioneer* printed a special issue. Bold headlines called attention to the killings. The story that followed cited the fact that W. C. Bernhart had died as a result of an injury that had taken place the day Huston and Luster had been killed.

Set in bold type, was another article:

Cowardly Note From the Killers

Sometime between midnight and 4 a.m., following the deaths of three prominent citizens of Ochoco Valley, an unsigned note bearing a skull and crossed bones was slipped under the front door of this newspaper. The message it contained stated that Schwartz and his two hired men (Huston and Luster) were part of a gang that had been running horses and cattle out of the county. It went on to say that anyone else caught rustling live-stock would be dealt with in the same manner.

An editorial, enclosed in a black border, was prominently displayed in the lower right- hand corner of the front page:

Like cowards in the night, a band of so-called vigilantes from the Ochoco Cattlemen's Protective Association struck; backshooting prominent McKay Creek Rancher A. L. Schwartz as he sat playing cards in Burmeister's Saloon.

After this foul deed was done, the same group of night riders then hung Charlie Luster and Sid Huston, and, in senseless violence, fired more than twenty shots into their already dead bodies.

W. C. Bernhart, local blacksmith and prominent member of the Cattlemen's Association, is believed to have been wounded by Luster, whose gun contained two spent cartridges.

It is also a belief of the editor of this paper that the earlier murder of Lucius Langdon and the hanging of W. H. Harrison were done by the same group of men.

These senseless killings must stop. This paper serves notice that we will be honest purveyors of the truth in reporting any further such lawless incidents, and will publish the names of those involved as they become known to us.

(signed) Robert O. Reich
Editor
The Ochoco Pioneer

Major Sid Duncan was at his home on Fourth and Claypool, where he was reading the *Review*. When he finished, he turned livid. The veins in his neck and forehead were swollen and pulsating. He threw the paper angrily at George Cotter, who had rushed over with a copy as soon as it hit the streets.

"Serves notice on us?" He shrieked at Cotter, his neck at a stiffer angle than usual due to his anger. "What does he mean serves notice? That pipsqueak. I'll serve notice on him. Just like I did the two Gale brothers in Roseburg. The ones that left this," he cursed, pointing at the lump in his neck where Sid Gale's bullet had lodged.

He reached for his revolver and cartridge belt that were hanging on an antler rack and buckled it around his thin waist. "Two seconds after I reach the *Pioneer*, they're going to need a new editor."

George Cotter rose quickly from the mohair stuffed chair in which he had been sitting and blocked Duncan's way.

"Now, now Major," he said soothingly, even though he was as upset as the diminutive Duncan. "It won't do any good to go off half-cocked. The town's too upset about Schwartz and the two boys for us to do something rash."

Duncan's deep set eyes flashed a warning. His right arm lifted.

For a moment Cotter thought Duncan intended to push by him, then the arm dropped.

"I hate to admit it, but you're right. I'll wait a few days, then take care of the skunk." Duncan's voice was full of fury.

"Maybe there's an even better way," he added. "I'll have a couple of my boys pay him a visit in a week or two. He won't be able to set type if he doesn't have any fingers left."

Seeing Cotter's startled expression, he gave a contemptuous laugh. Then as Cotter's face drained white, he sneered, "What's the matter, George. About to lose your breakfast over the thought of a few ink-stained fingers?"

CHAPTER SEVENTEEN

A heavy wind from the river played with a skeletal tumbleweed that rolled down the street, bouncing and circling until it was stopped by the plank sidewalk that ran in front of Prineville's weathered wooden buildings. Late afternoon shadows from buildings on the west side of Main cast their harsh imprint on the false fronts of the buildings facing them across the street.

Clay and Ellie Howard had just left R. Rowan and Sons Tinware and were passing the Wayne Saloon as they headed for home. Gil Wayne was standing in his doorway and tipped his hat to Ellie as they stopped to talk. A block down the street, Bob Reich, editor of the *Ochoco Pioneer*, bent to lock his front door.

Without warning, two men in range clothes came from the alley by the *Pioneer* and stopped behind the stooped newspaperman.

Gil was telling Clay about a new dance hall he was thinking of building when a shocked gasp from Ellie caught their attention. She grabbed Clay's arm and pointed up the street. "Clay, look!"

Bob Reich was being pistol whipped.

With an oath, Clay turned to move toward them. Wayne's huge hand gripped his arm, stopping him.

"Clay, what's happening is none of our business. We'd be better off not getting involved."

Ellie gave the saloon keeper a shocked look. Clay took a step back and knocked Wayne's hand away. His voice was measured and cold. "Gil, you've got to decide which

88

side of the fence you're on. And you can't wait any longer. What's it going to be?"

For several seconds, Wayne didn't answer. The conflict showed in a tick that pulled at the side of his mouth. A tumbleweed raced past them and sped toward the newspaper office as if rushing to help the embattled editor.

"Hurry, Clay. He's down and they're kicking him. He's not moving," Ellie pleaded.

The men's eyes locked. Then Wayne looked down. When he looked up, Clay could see a decision had been made.

"They're armed, and we're not. Just stay put until I get back." Wayne bolted into his saloon.

He reappeared just as Ellie screamed. One of the attackers had unsheathed a skinning knife and was forcing Reich's right hand flat on the heavy plank sidewalk. Clay was already racing to help.

The knife was poised over the editor's knuckles when the shotgun Wayne had gone for roared. He yelled out, "Jump aside, Clay. The next barrel isn't going into the air."

The two attackers froze, then cursed and dove for cover as buckshot splintered wood at the spot where they had been kneeling over the unconscious Reich.

"Don't bother to chase them, Clay," Gil Wayne yelled out, "I recognized them both."

"So did I," Clay shouted back. "They were Sid Duncan's hands. He'll have to answer for that."

By this time, a crowd had gathered. Three men who came from the Antler Cafe, Steve Staats, John Combs and Sam Smith, hurried to Clay Howard's side. They looked questioningly at Clay, who nodded and spoke just five words. "Tonight. 11:00 o'clock. My house."

Just after midnight, seven riders rode to the Duncan brothers' spread on Willow Creek. Joe Hanks and Duane

89

Law, the two men who had assaulted the editor, were pulled out of the bunkhouse and given their choice. Leave the country or stay and be hung. They chose to leave.

Once it had been a cougar's lair. Then it housed a nest of rattlesnakes. After that it was a coyote den.

It was a centuries-old erosion cut halfway up a lava cliff that overlooked Crooked River. Now it was being used as a shelter by the Rogers brothers and a hardcase named Marvin McArthur. It was the closest thing to a home any of them had ever known. Most nights they slept under the stars; a saddle for a pillow and a saddle blanket their bed.

For two weeks they had been hiding, eating beans and what small game they could kill. Tonight it was sage hen. Their coffee grinds had been watered down to the point there was no taste, and little color, left.

The four of them had been rustling horses in Crooked River Valley. Horses they planned on taking to Dry Lake, an exchange point east of Linkville in the Klamath country. But they had been ambushed by the Ochoco Cattlemen's Protective Association at the Goodman Ranch as they were cutting out a string of recently broken wild mustangs. During the encounter, McArthur had taken a bullet through his back. It shattered a rib and pierced one of his lungs. For the first week they couldn't build a fire because of the search parties looking for them. Their cramped quarters and McArthur's constant coughing had worked on the nerves of his three companions. Finally, one of them, Ted Rogers, the youngest brother, reached his breaking point. He picked up a burning juniper branch and thrust it inches from McArthur's face. "Damnit, Marvin, your hacking is driving me crazy. You've not let up since we holed up in this dump."

In answer, McArthur drew his Colt and pulled back the hammer, sniffed deeply to gather bloody phlegm in his throat, and spat at his antagonist. "Try it, Ted," he rasped. "If you want a bullet hole of your own."

Ted's older brother Rod grabbed the smoking piece of wood and stuck it back in the fire. "Are you crazy? That's all we need is to start shootin' at each other."

"Well, I've plain had it, Rod," Ted uttered a curse. "Stuck here with that shot-up cripple." He stood from the fire, his back bent to the low ceiling. "I'm gettin' out, and I'm getting out now."

Clarence, the middle brother, was two year's older than Ted and a year younger than Rod. He sat in front of the fire with his legs folded Indian-style. His eyes were blood red from the smoke that filled the small space they lived in. Looking at Rod he said, "I agree with Ted. We're livin' no better than wild animals. Nothin' to eat. No tobacco and no whiskey. I'm for movin' on." He cast a hateful glance at his sick companion. "And them that can't keep up will just have to stay behind."

McArthur knew how bad his wound was. The throbbing in his rib cage had stopped, but the smell of rotting flesh told him that gangrene had set in. He guessed he had a week at the most. Summoning his strength, he rose to one knee. "You know who put us here. The Cattlemen's Association. And here we sit, takin' it." His eyes flared with the fever that was burning him up. "You can light out with your tail 'tween your legs like a bitch dog, but I'm for putting the torch to Prineville before we leave. Give them something to remember us by."

His suggestion was met with complete silence. Then Clarence hopped around the oily fire like a frog, slapping his thigh and howling like a coyote. "Damned if that don't sound good to me. Pay 'em back for livin' in this hell hole."

Ted slapped his brother's back enthusiastically. "I'll go down to the set-back and get the horses right now. Meet me by the river." He started to leave, then stopped to look at his oldest brother. "All right with you Rod?"

Knowing that he neither could, nor wanted to stop them, Rodney Rogers nodded his agreement. "The Association knows we didn't get away and will be watching the Maury Mountain route. They won't expect us to go north." Caught up in the excitement of what was ahead, he said, "Let's do it. We'll set fire to that hick town, then head west toward the Deschutes and work our way south."

When the three met Ted by the ice-frozen bank of Crooked River he only had three horses with him.

"Where's my horse. Where's Black Ned?" Clarence asked.

"Broke his hobble I guess," Ted answered. "He wasn't with the rest. Too dark to see if he left any tracks, and we don't want to travel by day, that's for certain."

Rod strode to his tall chestnut. "You can ride double with me, Clary. We'll pick up another mount on our way. Ted, carry his saddle on your horse."

In two hours the four rustlers rode out of the last canyon that hid Crooked River and followed its banks on a trail that led to town. Clarence Rogers was now riding a mare. It carried a Lazy H brand. They had stolen it from one of Clay Howard's corrals less than an hour ago.

The four rustlers were in such a hurry to leave their hideout they had made no plans on what they would do when they reached Prineville.

Just south of town they stopped. After arguing a few minutes, the barking of nearby ranch dogs got on McArthur's nerves. "You can sit here jawin' and freezin' if you want. I'm going to find the nearest waterin' hole and get me a bottle of whiskey. And I don't intend to wait no longer." He spurred his buckskin and cantered toward town.

The three brothers, not sure what they should do, hesitated. Then Rod spoke. "What the hell. I could use a snort or two myself." They caught up with the bent-over, coughing figure and rode four abreast into town.

It was Kelley's where they stopped. They dismounted, entered the saloon, picked up a bottle and chose a table against the far wall where they could watch the front door.

A driver from the Circle O saw them arrive. He also noted Clay Howard's brand on one of the horses. Figuring the horse had probably been stolen, he hurried for the sheriff's office to find Norman Frazier.

In the saloon, whiskey was having its effect on the empty stomach and frame of mind of Marvin McArthur. He had downed three quick shots, turning more sullen with each drink. His fevered mind began playing tricks on him. As the three brothers bent over their glasses, their raspy whispers throbbed in his head, growing louder and louder. He covered his ears with both hands and jumped to his feet, upsetting their rough wooden table.

"I know what you're talking about," he shrieked. "You're planning on killing me." Jerking out his revolver he stepped sideways to a hanging kerosene lamp. "We were going to burn down this dump of a town, and now all's you can talk about is gunnin' down your partner."

With a sweep of his arm, he smashed the lantern. Coal oil splashed over his clothing and caught fire. Oblivious to the flames, his mind completely gone, he pointed his gun at the brothers, who sat in stunned silence.

Ted rose, his hands up, palms toward McArthur. "Hold on Mac, we . . ." He never had the chance to finish. Two shots hit him full in the chest.

A deafening roar followed. The demented outlaw was flung against the wall and collapsed on the floor, flames still licking at his shirt and pants. "Don't you two varmints move," Sheriff Frazier yelled from the door as he swung his sawed-off Greener at the two remaining Rogers brothers. "Sam," he said to the man at his side, nodding toward McArthur, "dump that bucket of sand by the stove on that varmint before he sets the whole place on fire."

Several men had followed Frazier into the saloon. Among them were Moe Cotter, Gus Brinkley and a bandaged Charley Conwell.

"Drag 'em out," yelled Conwell, pointing at Rod and Clarence Rogers. "We told the *Pioneer's* editor the Cattlemen's Association would hang the next bunch of rustlers we found, and that's what we're going to do. Right from the porch rafter in front of his door."

CHAPTER EIGHTEEN

When Tom Pickett got word from one of Clay's riders that a rustler had been shotgunned to death and two more were hung, he made a special trip to town.

He met Clay at the recently opened Ochoco Cafe.

"This sets us back, Tom," Clay was saying. "The Cattlemen's Association is all puffed up about their big capture and kill. And most of the decent townsfolk agree with them. It certainly does take the sting out of their previous murders. What adds insult to injury is that one of the thieves was riding a horse of mine!"

"Clay," Tom responded. "The rustlers got only what was coming to them. The bartender at Kelley's said the one who set himself on fire spilled the beans about their plans to put the torch to town. You know everyone is scared to death of a fire starting in any of these old buildings. What if they had?"

Clay sighed heavily. "I know, Tom. I don't fault what they did, although I don't go along with the hanging. They should at least have gotten a fair trial. I just fear this is going to make it harder for us to keep the vigilantes under control. The way they're talking now, they want to hang any stranger that rides into town."

"Have you talked to any of the others who think like us?" Tom asked.

"Yep. They feel the same as I do." He brightened up. "At least we know which direction Gil Wayne leans. However, he's made it plain to anyone who'll listen that he's not taking sides. Says he acted out of fair play to help Bob Reich and that he would have done the same for anyone."

"What about the other name on your undecided list, Clay?"

"You mean Bill Russell? I don't know yet, Tom. He's making all the right motions. My gut feeling is that there's a piece missing somewhere. I suppose we'll find out soon enough when the time comes."

"Say, what's the story on George Cotter and old man Gird?"

Tom's question brought a chuckle from Clay. Then an open laugh. "Don't tell me you haven't heard it?"

Tom shook his head. "Only that old man Gird made Cotter look like a darned fool."

"He sure did. Let me get us a refill and I'll tell you what happened."

Clay rose stiffly, grabbed the heavy china cups and went to the counter. He chatted a while with Jim Burns, the owner, then he came back, holding the steaming cups by their tops with his fingers. He set them down and vigorously shook both hands in the air. "One thing you can say for Burns, he keeps his coffee hot."

"O.K., Clay. I know your tactics too well. Quit stalling." Tom leaned back in his chair, a wide grin on his face. He loved Clay Howard as if the older man were his own father. And he knew Clay shared the same feeling. "It must be a good one if it takes you this long to get around to it."

Clay grinned and proceeded. "You knew George has been down on young Nate Gird because he wouldn't join the Cattlemen's Association. Anyway, Nate's dad and Origen Cotter had some horses on the range at shares. They branded them all with a 67. Origen branded his half on the stifle. Ben used the same iron, but put it on the shoulder.

"Young Nate went up to Combs Flat, where they kept them, to get one of his dad's horses. He knew his pa used the 67 brand, but not knowing the agreement, roped one of Cotter's horses instead. In trying to settle the horse down, he ran him into a badger hole and broke its leg. The horse was so crippled he had to shoot it."

Clay paused and shot a look at Tom's cup, "Want some pie with your coffee?"

Tom grinned. "No, I want to hear the rest of the story."

"O.K., then. Well, when George Cotter heard about his dad Origen's horse, he figured on nailing Nate for horse rustling. Swore out a warrant and had his lackey Frazier put Nate in jail. Then he went up to Combs Flat and cut a piece of hide off the dead horse to show it had Origen's brand on it.

"When a friend of ours heard about it he cut the same size chunk of hide off the shoulder, where Gird's brand would have been. Then he cut a little more off the stifle where Cotter had cut his patch, so Cotter's patch wouldn't match. When they held court, Cotter waved his piece of horsehide before the jury. Then Nate Gird jumps up and says, 'Hold on now. How does the jury know this came from the horse we're talking about?'"

"Cotter got all steamed and said 'Because I can prove it by the patch I'm holding.'"

"To make a long story short, the judge instructed the jury to ride out and take a look at the horse in question. Naturally, when they got there Cotter's patch didn't fit, and as the hide was missing where Ben Gird's mark would have been, the jury had to turn Nate loose on lack of evidence. George was fit to be tied."

Tom laughed until his stomach ached, then leaned toward Clay and, in a low voice asked conspiratorially, "That friend of ours wouldn't have been John Combs, would it?"

"Hard to say," said Clay, his grin growing. "It sounds like something he might do."

Tom got up to leave. "Best be making my way back, Clay. Give my best to Ellie. And keep me posted."

"Will do, Tom. Take care of yourself."

Before leaving, Tom made a stop at Senders' Mercantile. He had been thinking of Mary Kay Reed all the way in and wanted to tell her he had decided to go to the Grange dance. Whistling a toneless tune, he crossed the street and pushed open the door. As he closed it, he reached up to silence the jingling bell. It was the only thing about the store that bothered him.

Mary Kay was bent over a flour barrel, spooning some of the white powder into a paper sack. Her forehead was dusted where she must have touched it with the back of her hand to replace a strand of hair.

Tom stood, feet spread, watching her. He coughed slightly.

"Why, hello Tom," she said, looking up. "My word, this is twice you've been to town in the last three weeks."

Missing the touch of sarcasm in her voice, Tom blurted out, "Mary Kay, I've been thinking about the dance. I've decided to go."

"So. What has that got to do with me?" she asked, turning back to her job of repackaging the flour.

Tom flushed and shifted his feet. "Maybe. I thought. . ." Taking a deep breath, he exhaled sharply. "I thought I'd bring in the surrey. If you'd like to go with me."

Mary Kay swirled to look at him. Her ankle-length skirt caught some spilled flour and it hung suspended in the air. A mixture of emotions crossed her face, and the back of her hand went to her mouth, which hung open. She looked stricken.

"Tom," she began, then stopped, her breasts rising and falling as she took a deep breath to regain her composure. Then she stood, back erect. "Tom, I thought you didn't want to go to the dance, so I accepted Karl Miller's invitation to go with him."

It was Tom's turn to look stricken. He couldn't think of anything to say, so turned to leave.

With a sharp cry of pain, she rushed to him and held his arm. Then she reached for his hand and took it gently in her own. "I would have waited if I thought you might ask me. Just because he's taking me to the dance doesn't mean I have to dance every dance with him. I'll save some for you."

Tom replayed her last words over and over to himself as he rode back to his ranch. The next time he saw her he would be able to talk to her without tying himself in knots, because now he knew she felt the same way about him as he felt about her.

CHAPTER NINETEEN

After the hanging of the rustlers in January, the ranchers, homesteaders and townspeople turned all of their energy to surviving the late winter. The violence and killings of the previous year were shoved into the back of their minds. Even Clay Howard and the people listed in his ledger, many of whom he consulted frequently, felt the worst had passed. The only ones who didn't feel this way were the outspoken Mogan brothers, Frank and Mike. They took every opportunity to complain bitterly about the roughshod methods used by the Cattlemen's Association.

Late spring, a second newspaper made its appearance in Prineville. The *Prineville News*. The paper's editorials backed the Cattlemen's Association and took issue with Bob Reich's *Ochoco Pioneer* on just about every subject. Rumor had it that George Cotter and a silent investor were backing the *News*, but there was no concrete proof and both Cotter and the editor of the new weekly denied this was the case.

The community liked the idea of two newspapers that expressed different points of view. At his mercantile store, Lou Senders was proud of telling people passing through, as well as new arrivals, that Prineville would soon be the second largest city in the state. "Look at how we've grown," he took pleasure in saying. "From three stores a little over ten years ago to over forty business establishments now. You just watch. Prineville will be a big city yet. It's a fine place to settle and raise a family."

Senders had every reason to feel optimistic. Cattlemen were prospering and there was more than enough lush grazing land for all. Homesteaders were arriving almost daily and stages from the Willamette Valley, Klamath Basin and The Dalles passed through twice a week. Tethrow's ferry was now open across the Deschutes, connecting the county road to the Willamette Valley and Cascade Mountain Wagon Road that ran, unimpeded, to the Willamette Valley. This easy access created a lively exchange of goods between the areas east and west of the Cascades. Prineville was the connecting link and soon became the trading center for all of the smaller communities that dotted Central and Eastern Oregon.

There was even talk that a rail line was being considered by a man named Harriman from back east. It would cross the country to The Dalles, and end in Portland. Rumor had it a trunk line was planned that would run through Prineville to Fort Klamath and California.

Sawmills flourished along Mill and McKay Creeks, and high efficiency hydraulic mines were replacing the cruder placer mines that lined the stage road to Mitchell and Summit Prairie in the Ochocos.

Individual miners still worked the mountain streams by hand, however, and it was one of these, with his jenny mule, who made a find that was the main topic of conversation in Prineville for weeks. It also started a stampede for gold that was not to be found in the ground, or creeks, but in leather sacks.

In 1863, at the height of the gold strike at Canyon City, a group of masked men robbed a mining camp in the Washington Territory of a month's diggings of gold dust. They escaped on six horses. Two days later they robbed the bank in Dayville, on the John Day River. They were tracked through the Blue Mountains and the Mitchell desert to the Ochoco Mountains, a few miles northeast of Prineville, by Mill Creek road. Here their pursuers lost their trail.

It was only a mile from the spot the posse turned back that the miner found the remains of six saddle horses that had been tied to a fallen log. There were saddles but no saddlebags on the horses, which led to the theory the bandits had been panicked by the posse and fled on foot, burying their gold before they left.

Word of the miner's discovery spread like wildfire. Hordes of people who hoped to strike it rich descended on the area with picks and shovels, making the countryside look, as Lynn Wood the barber put it, "Like a bunch of badgers gone crazy, with dirt flying in the air and holes everywhere."

The gold was never found, and for weeks in the bars and on the streets, no one talked much about anything else.

In another month, the gold fever had passed and the community's attention turned to the Spring dance which was being held at the Grange Hall. The dance was the big social event of the year. Families who had been cooped up all winter were anxious to visit, exchange gossip and let their hair down.

The mercantile stores had been laying in new bolts of calico cloth, anticipating the run they expected from women making new dresses for themselves and their daughters. Lynn Wood sharpened all of his barber shears and was busy from morning 'til late at night. In those communities surrounding Prineville, men, urged on by their wives, greased their wagon wheels and replaced worn-out springs for the trip to town..

Finally, the big day arrived. Every road into Prineville was lined with buckboards, wagons and surreys. There were shouted greetings as the faster vehicles passed slower ones. The excitement in the air was infectious, as these usually reserved people whooped with laughter. Most of the wagons carried picnic baskets loaded with baked goods for the dance supper.

Tom Pickett, on his way to town, met Billie Adams and his family where Ochoco Creek intersected the dirt road from the Maury Mountains. He pulled his horse alongside their old Conestoga that had been converted into a flatbed wagon and exchanged greetings as they rode, catching up on what each of them had been doing the past year. The Adamses had a homestead on upper Beaver Creek, but Tom knew Billie was more interested in ranching than farming. Adams had built a small herd and all of his spare cash went into buying breed cows. Tom asked, in the course of the conversation, how Billie's herd was coming along.

"Everything was going fine until a month ago," Billie exploded. "I lost six head to rustlers last month. But I wasn't the only one. Slim Peterson on Wolf Creek and March Logan on the north fork of Crooked River also had some taken."

"Are you sure they were rustlers, Billie? Maybe they just wandered off."

"They were rustlers all right. Slim, March and I tracked them as far as the Walker Mountains, then lost their trail in the swampy area by Fort Klamath. I got an idea who took 'em, too. That Rosslyn bunch. Word is they're operating out of the Klamath Basin area."

"I'm sorry to hear about your loss, Billie. Anything I can do?"

"Nothin' anybody can do. They're gone. But there's one thing I'm going to do and that's for sure. Soon as I reach Prineville I'm looking up George Cotter and joining the Cattlemen's Association. Up to last month, I haven't cared much for their high-handed ways. But up to last month I hadn't had any stock rustled either."

103

Billie's wife, Ruth, put her hand on her husband's arm and spoke gently. "Now Billie, you promised you wouldn't get all riled up on this trip. What's done is done and fretting won't help. We're here to visit and enjoy the dance."

Tom addressed them both. "I'm sorry for bringing the subject up, Billie. I hadn't heard. When I said if there's anything I can do, I meant it. If you need some breed cows or a bull, just let me know." Touching the brim of his hat with his fingers, he addressed Mrs. Adams. "Ma'am," he said, then spurred his horse and rode on ahead.

No one could possibly miss where the dance and social were being held. Tom just followed the procession of people to the imposing, false-fronted two-story wooden hall at Second and Claypool. It was a building built by The Independent Order of Oddfellows for their lodge, but it was also used by the Masons, Eastern Star and the Grange for their meetings. The Grange used it so much that it was more often referred to as the Grange Hall than the I.0.0.F building.

Tom paused to watch the crowd. There was activity everywhere. People mingled to visit while others un-loaded food from their wagons. Children, happy to have found new playmates, screamed and chased each other. Their high-pitched shrieks punctuated the more sedate but happy voices of their elders.

Tom's conversation with Billie Adams bothered him. But Billie's wife was right. What was done was done and couldn't be redone. People were here to enjoy themselves. And so would he. With that decision made, his spirits rose and he began looking for Mary Katherine Reed.

He had about given up hope of finding her in the milling crowd and was just lifting a leg to dismount when the jingling of harness bells caught his attention. He settled back. Then a shiny, newly painted black surrey caught his eye. It was driven by two matched dappled greys. Tom glanced at the driver to see who it was. Sitting proud and erect in the seat, reins held properly in both hands, was Karl Miller.

Miller was wearing a dark wool suit and white shirt with a black string tie. A royal blue vest was accessorized with a gold nugget watch chain. Tom could see one of Miller's boots, which was braced on the surrey. It was shiny and new, with hand tooling that shouted their expense. On his head sat an unweathered Stetson hat.

Tom swallowed hard as he glanced at his new jeans, and 'go to town' boots that were scuffed but clean and free of mud. His wool shirt and plain leather vest suddenly felt shabby and inadequate. It wasn't until that morning that he'd decided what he was going to wear. Now he was sorry he hadn't given it more thought.

Looking toward the surrey again, he glanced at the passenger side. If Tom was taken aback by Dutch Miller's appearance, he was stunned by the sight of Mary Kay. Her radiant beauty made Miller and the greys look pale by comparison. Those who spotted the rig and its occupants gasped at the commanding sight, then nudged their neighbors.

Wrapping the reins around the brake lever, Miller jumped down and hurried around the front of the horses to assist Mary Kay.

As she stood, Tom felt his heart turn over in his chest. Mary Kay's eyes were dancing with excitement, and her face was flushed, showing its pleasure; and, Tom guessed, probably pride at the manner in which she had arrived at the dance. Her auburn hair had been brushed until it shone, and full curls hung over bare shoulders, complementing the length of hair that draped her back. Her dress was green velvet, tied at her slim waist with a matching sash. As she lifted a leg to alight, Tom couldn't help but stare at her slim ankle and dainty foot which was encased in a brocade dancing slipper.

Before leaving the surrey, she glanced quickly over the crowd. Seeing Tom, her face blossomed in a smile and she held his eyes for several seconds. Karl Miller had been holding her arm to help her. He followed the direction of her gaze and when he saw Pickett pulled at her elbow impatiently. She nodded to him graciously, lifted her skirt and jumped lightly to the ground. Karl, large and imposing, offered his arm and they turned to acknowledge the greetings they were receiving.

Tom's first impulse was to forget the dance and go home. He was no match for Karl Miller in all of his finery. How could he possibly ask Mary Kay to dance, she being so dressed up and all. He was just about to turn his horse and leave when Clay Howard grabbed his reins at the bit and stroked the horses muzzle.

"You've been sitting there fifteen minutes, Tom. Don't you think it's time you got off your horse?"

Clay's face grinned up at him. He had seen Tom watching Mary Kay.

Tom's face flushed a deep red, "I don't know Clay. I was thinking of going home. I'm not really dressed for the occasion."

Clay had seen Miller arrive too, and read Tom's mind. He laughed in good humor. "Look around. You're better dressed than most of the folks here. Get down. I'll take care of your horse."

Tom paused momentarily, then did as he was told. As soon as his feet hit the ground, Clay slapped him on the arm affectionately. "Now go say hello to Ellie. She's been waiting to see you." Before he had a chance to answer, Clay led his horse away.

After he had shared a potluck supper with the Howards, Gil Wayne, and Gil's wife and their four children, Tom sat quietly, listening to the small talk of the two families.

When the music started in the I.O.O.F. building, Clay looked over at Tom. "Don't let us hold you up, Tom. A fellow your age should be dancing, not talking about quilts and the new Union Church."

Self-consciously, Tom rose, thanked Ellie and Gil's wife Anna for providing supper, and made his way to the hall's double-doors that were flanked by two large glass windows.

Straw had been spread on the floor and twenty couples were dancing to music from the trio of musicians on the lodge's raised platform: Mike Friedman at the piano, Stew Ritchie and his violin and Tom McClaren playing his three-stringed banjo. The usual group of single men were bunched in a corner, waiting for the dance to end so they could choose a partner. Occasionally, one would cut in, at the annoyance of the male whose dance was interrupted. Now and then they left the hall in groups of two's and three's, to return a few minutes later with flushed faces and sheepish grins. Tom knew what was happening. They were sampling some of Jim Teevan's white lightning behind the building.

As the rotating bodies swung by he spotted Karl Miller and Mary Kay. Miller was shuffling, stumbling awkwardly as he tried to keep time to the music. Mary Kay caught Tom's eye and gave him a pleading look. The next time they came around, Tom stepped forward and tapped Miller on the shoulder.

"Mind if I take a turn, Dutch?"

Miller stopped and gave him a hateful look. "Find yourself another partner."

Fearing that a scene might develop, Mary Kay spoke up quickly. "The next dance can be yours, Tom."

With a hard look at them both, Miller said, "Maybe one's all right."

Tom stared back and replied, "I think that's up to the lady to decide."

"She came with me. It's for me to decide." Then Miller swung Mary Kay away in a flatfooted two-step.

The music stopped and Miller guided Mary Kay to the other side of the room. Tom hesitated, then as the musicians struck up a quadrille, he hurried over.

As they joined the circle of dancers, Mary Kay took his hand and whispered, "He'll never admit it, but I think you did him a favor. I'm sure he's never square-danced before."

Tom had no time to answer as they lined up with another couple and bowed to their partners.

Before he knew it the dance was over. A flushed and happy Mary Kay held his arm tightly as they left the floor. She again whispered an aside. "Wait a dance or two for a slower number." She squeezed his hand as they reached Karl Miller.

Three dances later, as the strains of 'Mary-Come-a-Waltzing' filled the large wood-framed building, Tom approached the two again. He had noticed that Karl had brusquely refused to let anyone else dance with Mary Kay. She appeared tense and looked at him nervously as he asked her for the dance. Before she could reply, Miller jabbed a thick, blunt finger on his chest.

"I said one was all right. No more."

Taken aback, Tom looked at Miller then at Mary Kay. He read the unhappy look in her eyes. Suddenly he knew that the vivacious happy girl he had seen entering the dance was now downright miserable. His temper flared.

"Dutch, take your finger off my chest or you'll be pointing at things with a stub."

Miller's breathing stopped. His neck and face swelled with a hot rage. The air came out of his lungs with a burst and he drew back and cocked a huge fist, intending to smash Tom's face.

Mary Kay sensed what was happening and stepped between them.

"Karl! Tom! Stop this at once!" She turned to her escort.

"Karl, when I accepted your invitation I assumed you would accord me the courtesy of letting me dance with other people." Her eyes snapped. "I'm not one of your mine hands to be bossed around."

Miller responded to her argument like he did every confrontation. In a bull-headed manner, a gift of his Dutch ancestry, he replied, "I am leaving this dance and you are leaving with me, Mary Katherine."

"Karl," Mary Kay replied softly, "you can leave if you like, but I am not leaving with you. In fact," her voice caught, "even if you stay I am not leaving with you." She turned to Tom. "I think you were about to ask me to dance." She quickly led him to the floor and slipped into his arms.

Over her shoulder Tom saw Karl Miller stomp from the room, roughly pushing aside anyone who got in his way.

Speechless, Tom looked at his partner, still stiff from her anger, and held her closer. As she melted in his arms he looked down at her. "You know, you're a perfect fit," he said.

"Oh, Tom," she replied, leaning into him and resting her head on his shoulder. "What have I done?"

"You've saved me from getting a broken jaw is what you've done," he laughed, swinging her gaily among the other couples on the dance floor.

CHAPTER TWENTY

As summer passed, Tom found himself using any excuse to make the trip to town to see Mary Kay. Finally, Arne Swenson, the usually jovial 3C cook, openly began complaining because he wasn't able to break the dull routine of baking and cooking three meals a day to make an occasional trip to Prineville to pick up supplies. Reub Hassler even idly suggested one day that they probably would see more of Tom if they moved their cattle to where Marks Creek joined Ochoco Creek—six miles west—because that was the trail Tom took to town. That way they at least would have the chance to wave to him once in a while. To this remark one hand replied, "He's travelled that route so much it looks like a cattle run. You can see his dust for miles."

Even Clay Howard jokingly told Tom that he and Ellie had seen more of him in the last month than they had the previous three years.

The Senders, especially, went out of their way to make Tom feel at home. And even though he often arrived unannounced many afternoons, there was always a place set for him at the table. After dinner, Martha Senders would discreetly suggest to her husband Lou that there was inventory that needed to be checked in the store downstairs, or accounts they should bring up to date. Then they would excuse themselves.

They took pleasure in seeing Mary Kay so happy. In truth, as they never had been able to have children, they looked upon her as their own flesh and blood daughter.

On weekends, Tom and Mary Kay loved to explore the country together and would spend hours in the areas around Steen's Pillar, Lamonta Community and the chimney-like rocks that looked down on Crooked River. On clear evenings they often rode to the tall rimrocks just west of town where they watched the sun set over the splendor of the Cascade Mountains.

Other evenings they would ride to the butte named after Origen Cotter to watch the sun throw stippled patches of gold and orange on the pine belted ridges of the Ochoco range east of them.

One Sunday, after staying in town the night before, Tom rented a one-horse rig from the stables and they drove up the rutted road that led to Mitchell and by Tom's spread. When they stopped at the ranch house for a picnic lunch Arne Swenson insisted he fix, they were subjected to a lot of good-natured ribbing from the hands who were there. Both of them took it in good spirits—the way it was intended. Everyone at the ranch knew and respected Mary Kay, and to the last man they were pleased at the relationship that was developing between the two.

As they were preparing to leave for the trail that led to Lookout Mountain, Reub Hassler came forward. He removed his stained and weathered hat with one hand. The other held a wicker basket covered with a gingham cloth that he placed on the back seat. He awkwardly twisted the Stetson by its brim with both hands.

"I rightly don't know how to say this," he coughed nervously, looking at the half-dozen cowpokes arranged behind him for support, then back at Mary Kay. "I just. . . that is we just want you to know your visit perked us up a bit. Shucks, I guess what I'm trying to say is, we all hope you'll come visit more often." Reub looked straight at his feet. His face and neck turned a bright shade of pink.

"Why, Reub," Mary Kay replied gently, reaching down to touch his shoulder. "That's the nicest compliment I have ever been paid. Thank you. I hope I will too. I look forward to it."

Tom quirted the spirited mare and as they left Mary Kay turned to wave. Most shuffled their feet. Two raised their arms then quickly dropped them, afraid they would be kidded about being too soft.

"You know, Tom, your men think a lot of you," Mary Kay said as they rounded a bend in the valley and the ranch houses disappeared from sight.

"And I think a lot of them. Particularly Reub. The two of us have been through some pretty tight times together."

They rode on in silence, skirting the stand of birch that spread along a willow-lined creek in which beaver were busily improving their dams; too concerned in finishing their work to bother with the passing couple.

Mary Kay reached out to take Tom's free hand. A gentle breeze rearranged her hair, forming a halo effect around her face that was backlighted by the sun. "What do you suppose God was thinking of when he created this country?" she asked softly.

"Why, I suppose he was thinking of us, and that one day we would be riding through asking that very same question."

"Oh, Tom," she said in mock-anger, releasing his hand and pushing his arm playfully. "That's blasphemy. You're hopeless." Leaning her head against his shoulder, she asked, "Where are you taking me?"

"Just over that ridge. To a surprise place."

They rode diagonally up a side hill. The horse moved easily over the carpet of pine needles, occasionally dislodging a fat cone that rolled down the slope. As they topped the draw, Tom pulled to a stop. "Here it is."

112

Mary Kay gasped at the sight. "Tom, it's beautiful!" She stood in the wagon, spellbound. Lookout Mountain soared above them, forming a perfect backdrop for a lush meadow lined with aspen whose shaking leaves reflected rays of dappled sunlight. A gentle stream coursed its way lazily the length of the valley that sheltered this verdant spot of land. The entire setting was ringed by gentle slopes of fir and pine; their shades of light and dark greens blending the meadow and mountain into a single picture.

"Oh look!" Mary Kay exclaimed in delight as she pointed at a small herd of grazing deer. "Three doe and their fawns. And there's a buck, behind that old juniper tree. Isn't he beautiful." This last remark was a statement, not a question.

The antlered buck, hearing the sound of her voice raised his head, studied them for a full minute, twitched his tail and resumed grazing.

"Did you see that, Tom? It's like he knows we belong here. And he accepts us."

Tom helped her from the surrey, then gently cradled her face in both of his hands. "We do belong here. That's why I brought you. If it's agreeable to you, this is where we'll build our home."

Tears welled in her eyes as she leaned forward and kissed him, throwing her arms tightly around his neck. "You know it's agreeable with me, Tom. I hope we will always be as happy as we are right now."

CHAPTER TWENTY ONE

The following Sunday after services at the Union Church, Tom and Mary Kay were surrounded by well-wishers, all intent on congratulating the bride-to-be. They all but ignored the flustered bridegroom, who had literally been torn from his fiancee's side.

Seeing Tom's discomfort, Mary Kay pushed her way to him and, taking him by the hand, they ran down the street, stopping only when they were well away from their friends. Mary Kay looked at Tom impishly, "If you could only have seen your face." She rose on tiptoes and kissed his cheek. Tom embarrassedly looked out of the corner of his eyes to see if anyone was watching. The sheepish expression on his face and his subvert glance made her laugh aloud. "Oh, Tom. We don't have to hide how we feel about each other anymore. I love you and I don't care who knows it."

"But Mary Kay," said Tom blushing. "Folks just normally don't go around kissing each other on the street. It's not proper."

"Oh? It's not proper is it? Then let's really give them something to talk about." She held his face in both hands and kissed him fiercely on the mouth. Then she picked up the skirts of her hooped Sunday dress and hurried down the sidewalk toward home.

Tom stood perfectly still, trying to maintain his composure as he again glanced toward the church. He fully expected to see everyone laughing and pointing at him. What he saw was a group too involved in talking to each other to even have noticed them. With a visible sigh of relief he hurried after Mary Kay.

She was waiting by the store's front door, a twinkle in her eyes. When he arrived she drew him inside, closed the door and threw herself in his arms. He held her close as she raised her face to his. "I do, you know."

"Do what?" he asked

"Love you, you idiot." They kissed long and tenderly.

Mary Kay pulled back and looked deeply into Tom's eyes. "Did I tell you the Senders left early this morning to visit some friends at Lamonta?"

"No, I guess you forgot. When will they be back?"

"Not until late tonight."

The rhythm of the horses, the dry heat from the sun and the slow moving silver ribbon of water that reflected its light off the ancient weathered cliffs, lulled them to silence.

"*Paga Tubic*," Tom drawled, looking at the snakelike stream that worked its way south.

"*Paga* who?" Mary Kay asked.

These were the first words either had spoken for the last half hour. They were comfortable enough just being together. Words weren't necessary.

"*Tubic. Paga Tubic.* That's what the Shoshone Indians called this river."

"What a lovely name," Mary Kay replied. "That's much more romantic than Crooked River."

After a pause she asked, "What were the Shoshone doing in Oregon? Their tribe is mostly to the east. On the west side of the Rockies—in the Washington Territory."

"They came with the Hudson's Bay Company as scouts to help the trappers. Quite a few stayed. Eventually they learned to speak Chinook as everyone else did at the time. It was a jargon the different tribes used to communicate with each other when they met to trade. When the first explorers, fur traders, missionaries and settlers arrived, they learned it, too. If there was no Chinook word for something, they mixed in their own French or English, which the Indians picked up in turn. Then the French Canadians contributed their dialect. Some Chinook jargon imitates the sounds of what they describe; like *quak* for a duck, or *tik tik* for watch. There are no more than five hundred words in all."

"Can you speak it, Tom?"

"Not very well. I only know a few words."

When he said nothing further, she pleaded, "Tell me the words you know, Tom."

"You should talk to preacher Neese. He speaks it fluently. When he first started missionary work he had to translate his prayers into a language the Indians could understand. It's tough because some words can have as many as twenty different meanings, depending on how you use them. *Hee hee* means laughter. *Hiyu hee hee* is plenty laughter, or very funny. But when *hiyu* is used with *muck-a-muck*, which is eat, it means much to eat."

Tom frowned, trying to recall more jargon he had heard. "The Indians use the word *puss puss* for cat, which is of English origin. But when they refer to a real mountain cat, a cougar, they added the Chinook word *hyas*. So *hyas puss puss* means big cat.

"Some words are fairly logical when you think about them. *Moos-moos* means cattle. *Howya* is a shortened version of how are you, or hello. But if you add *kla* before *howya*, this means goodbye. Not logical unless you know *kla* means the opposite of the word that follows."

"Tom," Mary Kay said, her face turning serious. "We've never discussed Indians much before. I guess it's because my family was killed by them." She hesitated, then went on. "I know they killed your parents, a

116

grandparent and two sisters when you were twelve. Do you hate them?"

Tom chose his words carefully. The muscles in his jaw hardened. "My family were massacred by the Columbia River Cayuse. A supposedly friendly tribe that got fired up by some malcontent medicine man and went on the warpath. No, I don't hate them Mary Kay. There are bad apples in every race. The white men can be just as violent. A copper skin doesn't automatically label someone as a savage and killer. You and I just happened to be in the wrong place at the wrong time."

"I'm glad to hear you say that, Tom. I was just four when my family were murdered and mutilated. Being so young, and away from home, I didn't see their bodies. This probably made a difference. And Paulina was killing everyone. Even his own people." Her voice lowered to a faint whisper. "Maybe it was fate, Tom. You could have still been farming on the Columbia, and I might have been stuck in the John Day Valley. We may have never met." She held out her hand for his, their touch giving each comfort. "Maybe it was planned this way," she said wistfully.

In his quiet way, Tom replied. "Fate can play a lot of tricks, Mary Kay. Take a murdering savage like Paulina. A being with no compassion. His very soul filled with hate. Now that he's dead the white man has honored him by naming a town, mountain, valley, lake, several creeks, a mountain peak and a prairie after him. Places of beauty. It doesn't make much sense."

He squeezed Mary Katherine's hand, tipped back his hat and leaned sideways to kiss her. "The only thing that makes sense is that out of the millions of people on earth, we found each other."

A resounding crash startled them both. Tom had to rein in their frightened horses. Once the animals had settled down they both looked to see what had happened.

A fat beaver was waddling away from a large Douglas fir that he had chewed through. Mary Kay put her hand to her mouth and snickered. Tom laughed uproariously.

"He must have been working on that giant all summer," Tom choked. "And talk about fate. If he planned to drop that tree in the river, he felled it the wrong way. That's probably why he's leaving. I wonder what his wife will say when he gets home."

"She'll probably bring his slippers, fix him dinner and not say anything, like a good wife would do."

"Tell you what," said Tom, pulling at the thong that held the wagon lariat. "Let's give him a hand!"

They improvised a singletree from a stout branch and hooked the horses to it. Tom then attached an end of his rope to the top of the fir and he, with Mary Kay guiding the horses, swung the tree around and into the stream. When they finished, they fell into the soft grass by the river, gasping for breath.

"*Hiyu hee hee,*" Mary Kay couldn't resist saying, which doubled them both over in laughter as they fell into each others arms.

For an hour they had lain together, absorbing the warmth of the sun and enjoying the spicey smells of sage and juniper. The sounds of nature held them to its bosom.

Mary Kay raised up on one arm and glanced at the river. "Look, Tom." There was excitement and pleasure in her voice.

Tom lifted himself by his elbows. The beaver who had felled the tree was back, gnawing at a crucial branch that would help block the stream's flow of water. On the bank was a small brown beaver watching his progress.

"Don't you wish all problems could be solved that easily?" Mary Kay said.

"Sometimes they are. When we're in the right place at the right time," Tom replied. He glanced at the sun.

"We have another hour, then we'd better start back. Have you ever seen the tree with the trap growing in it?"

"No," said Mary Kay eagerly. "Show it to me." She jumped to her feet and took both of his hands, pulling him up. When he was standing she hugged him. "I'm so happy when I'm with you, Tom. I never knew anyone could feel this way."

Tom couldn't find the right words, so he said nothing. It was hard for him to verbally express how he felt. He just hoped she understood his love for her was as deep as her love was for him.

Twenty minutes later Tom pointed to a chain that was completely imbedded in a live fir. A rusted trap dangled from its free end. "There it is. Left as a sign, I expect. The story goes it was put there in 1825 by a trapper who worked for Peter Skene Ogden. They worked a lot harder than we do to make a living. Each trapper was usually responsible for carrying six heavy beaver traps. In the winter they would chip a hole in the ice and dive to the bottom where they set their traps with musk bait. Each day they would have to go back under the ice to see if they had caught anything. The old-timers said it got so cold that sometimes the hole froze over before they could get out. I don't know whether that's true or not, but I do know it doesn't take water long to freeze solid in this valley in winter.

"About all the trappers had to eat was dried split peas, game jerky and hardtack. There are still a few of their muskets around town that they traded. You can tell them by the dragon and serpent etched on the breach. Also some of the best skinning knives to be found. They are called Sheffields because they came from a town by that name in England. People who have one swear they keep the best edge of any knife they ever owned.

"Most of the trappers came from Scotland," Tom continued. "Barney Prine knew one who settled near

119

Prineville. Barney claims the man told him jumping in a frozen river was no colder than being outside on a rainy day in the Highlands, only here he got paid for it."

Tom turned quiet. Seriously quiet. He looked at his work-roughened hands. "Mary Kay, you must think I'm a darned fool. I've been blabbing away most of the day."

"Tom, the last thing anyone would take you for is a fool. You know this country and you love this country. I enjoy hearing you tell about its history." She came to him, put her right hand behind his head and bent her face to him. "Today has been the second happiest day of my life."

Tom drew back, a puzzled look on his face. "When was your happiest day?"

"Oh Tom, you *are* hopeless. The day you asked me to marry you, of course."

CHAPTER TWENTY TWO

Summer slipped quickly into fall, and soon it was winter, but not the mild winter of the year before. By the end of September two feet of snow had fallen. At first, it was a blessing to the farmers and ranchers who now had time to catch up on all the indoor chores they had been neglecting all year. Harness was mended, wagon wheels were greased and restrapped with leather, and barns, outbuildings and homes were repaired or added on to. Barns and outbuildings had first priority, of course, because these protected the animals; the settlers' main source of income and food.

On Thanksgiving day all tasks were put aside. Families jammed into the two-room unpainted frame school house to see the pupils enact their annual pageant: the landing of the Pilgrims on Plymouth Rock, and the feast they prepared to celebrate their first year of survival. The sight of friendly Indians bringing gifts of food brought chuckles of amusement from the crowd, most of whom had spent their first years fighting savage bands of Paiutes, Snakes and Rogues. These Indians had been takers, not givers. And they certainly didn't come bearing food. But the audience went along with the version the students took from their history books. They whistled and yelled in glee as a friendly Indian chief presented John Alden with a live turkey that promptly wiggled out of Alden's grasp and raced around the room, gobbling wildly as it sought a means of escape. It was finally cornered and caught by two members of the cast. The only other mishap was when Priscilla said, "If you want my hand in marriage, speak for yourself, John." Twelve-year-old Jimmie Hawkins who was spending his second year in the fourth grade, and was playing John Alden, forgot what to say. After a long delay he cast a desperate look at the teacher, who loudly whispered his lines. The show ended with a scarlet-faced Hawkins being kissed on the cheek by the girl playing the part of Priscilla Mullens.

The students who played the part of the Indians were chosen because they had shaven skulls that were stained purple by Gentian Violet, a medicine used for the treatment of head lice.

The weekend following the school play, John Combs, Jeb Stuart and Steve Staats were in Kelley's Saloon having a nightcap after a visit with the Howards. They had asked Clay to join them but he begged off saying that he enjoyed his Saturday nights at home with Ellie. "Besides," he kidded them good naturedly, "I like to spend my Sundays feeling good, not nursing a hangover. Age does that, you know," he had added with a twinkle in his eyes.

Both Stuart and Combs were in a positive frame of mind and were trying to convince Staats he should be less pessimistic about the future.

"You've got to admit, Steve," Jeb Stuart was telling his friend, "the Cattlemen's Association has been on good behavior since they hung the Rogers boys and that feller McArthur. Other than some loud talk, they've left us pretty much alone."

"I don't know," Staats replied. "I feel like something's going to happen. From spring to fall they're busy tending to their cattle and looking for new members to join their organization. Then when winter sets in all hell breaks loose. Think back," he said earnestly, "their killings have taken place from December through March. Lucius Langdon and W. H. Harrison were killed a year ago last March; Sid Huston, Charley Luster and Al Schwartz last

Christmas eve. The attack on Bob Reich of the *Pioneer* was in January, the same month they hung the rustlers." He slapped the table with the flat of his hand. "I don't trust 'em. They don't have much to do when the snow falls, 'cept drink and cause trouble. For my money, now's the time we should really be on our guard."

Staats analysis sobered his two companions.

"Steve, I hope you're wrong," said John Combs, leaving a fifty-cent piece on the table as he rose to leave. "I guess all we can do is wait and see."

At four a.m., the last week in November, a flue fire started in the old Culver hotel, now renamed the Occidental. Before the volunteer fire department could rally and respond with their handpulled six-man pumper, the fire had spread to the dry wooden buildings that adjoined the hotel. By the time the volunteers got the flames under control, pumping water furiously from a hose thrown into Crooked River, the hotel, Kelley's Furniture Emporium and Mrs. Hobart's Millinery had burned completely to the ground. The fire was stopped at Selling and Brown's store, but not before most of their merchandise had been smoke-damaged.

The heat from the fire was so intense that most of those who fought it lost their eyebrows and all had their hair or beards singed. Those who formed the bucket brigade soon began slipping and falling as they tried to stand in mud that, hours earlier, had been solidly frozen ground.

It was a loss for Prineville and the people who owned the buildings, but the fire fighters could take heart from the fact their efforts had spared the rest of the town.

The next editions of Prineville's two newspapers gave full details on how the fire started. They commended the fire department volunteers as well as the citizens of

Prineville whose efforts had averted "total disaster." Praise was lavish.

Only the *Prineville News*, the paper whose editorials supported the Cattlemen's Association, ran a full page notice on its back cover. The notice stated the Association had decreed that anyone who had stock would need a permit before they could move cattle to the Blue Mountain range the following spring. The declaration was signed by Major Duncan.

Mike Mogan was with his brother Frank in the Ochoco Cafe. He had just finished reading this announcement. He roared in rage, his florid face in full flare of temper. Slamming his fist on the paper, he looked up and faced his older brother who had been reading over his shoulder.

"That's the last straw. We've been ranging in the Blues for five summers and never needed a pass before." A string of curses followed. "Bill Russell ain't buying this pass business and neither are we."

"Settle down, Mike," Frank replied. "Before we go off half-cocked let's get together with Clay Howard and those who think like us. We need to talk it over before we do anything rash."

"I say all we've done so far is talk," his brother shot back. "It's time to take some action. That runt Duncan needs to be called on this and I'm in the mood to do it."

Their conversation had not gone unnoticed. One of Major Duncan's hands slipped quietly out of the restaurant to report to his boss. He reached the Major's house and knocked on the front door. Duncan peered out through the bevel-edged glass window. When he saw who it was, he reached for the ornate brass handle and pulled the door open. He smelled whiskey on his rider's breath.

"What brings you to my home at this time of day, Gene?" he asked, his face cold and expressionless, thinking the man might have taken enough Dutch courage from the bottle to brace him for better wages.

"Thought you might like to know the Mogans are down at the Ochoco Cafe raisin' Cain about the notice in the *News.*"

Duncan's eyes narrowed. "They don't happen to be mentioning any names do they?"

"Yep, yours mainly. Want me to round up some of the boys and shut them up?"

"Not necessary, Gene. I'll see that the problem is taken care of." As an afterthought he asked, "Anyone else there?"

"Only Moe. I was having coffee with him."

"Ask Moe to meet me right away at Wayne's Saloon, then head on back to the ranch."

Gene paused to ask a question, thought better of it and left.

Duncan returned to the living room, got his hat and glanced at his belt and revolver that hung on a wall peg. He studied it a moment, made a decision and pulled out the pistol, leaving the belt. He tucked the gun in his pants, under his frock coat.

Moe Cotter was waiting at the bar when Duncan pushed open the batwing doors. He stopped and looked around, checking the occupants. Other than Gil Wayne, who was busy behind the counter, only two others were present; homesteaders whose wives were in town shopping. They were passing the time having a beer.

Wayne was stacking some glasses and had his back to Duncan, who caught Moe's eye and jerked his head to a corner table at the rear of the saloon.

"I'll take a beer, Gil," Duncan called out as he came to the bar. Handing over his nickel, he called out to Cotter. "Mind if I join you Moe, or would you rather be left alone?"

Confusion spread over Cotter's face. He didn't understand the game Duncan was playing with the bartender. "But I thought you wanted to see. . ." He never got to finish.

Duncan interrupted quickly. "That's right. I wanted to see what you've been up to lately." He sidestepped an empty table to reach Moe, irritated at Cotter's slow-witted response. Then he reminded himself that was why he had asked Moe to meet him in the first place. Who better to do the job he had in mind than the mentally retarded brother of George Cotter.

Seating himself opposite the broad-shouldered, barrel-chested Moe, he glanced at Cotter's glass. It was almost empty. He called out to Wayne again. "Gil, bring over a bottle of whatever young Moe here is drinking."

As the bottle was set before them, he picked up the whiskey and filled Moe's glass.

"Here's to you," he said raising his own mug of beer.

Moe downed the contents in one gulp. Duncan refilled his glass.

"What'd you want to see me about?" Moe's voice was slurred by the effect of an afternoon of hard drinking.

"I understand the Mogans have been complaining about needing grazing passes."

"In the Ochoco Cafe. And here, too," Moe replied. "They just left. Good thing, too. I was about to get up and bust their heads."

"I've got a better idea, Moe. But it calls for another drink." He raised his mug and took a short swallow. Moe put his glass to his lips and drained it.

Duncan leaned closer. "Here's your chance to get even with Mike, Moe."

"Get even? What do you mean get even?" An uncomprehending look filled Moe's eyes.

"Because of what he has been saying about you."

"Saying about me? What has he been saying about me?" A belligerent look spread over his puffy face.

Duncan leaned back, a mock-expression of surprise on his face.

"Why, you know Moe. What he tells everyone."

Still confused, and now angry, Moe asked, "What do you mean. What does he tell everyone?"

Looking around, as if he didn't want anyone else to hear, Duncan leaned forward and put both arms on the table. Bending his back, he hunched toward Moe.

"That you're a half-wit. An idiot. That you couldn't pour water out of a boot even if the directions were on the heel. We know that isn't so, Moe," Duncan purred. "But that's what Mike Mogan keeps telling everyone."

A blind rage came over Cotter. His face gorged with blood and his bull neck strained at his collar, the artery in his neck pumped furiously. He jumped to his feet, knocking over his chair. Drinks spilled over the table. "He said that," he roared, an insane look in his eyes. "I'll kill the son of a bitch for that kind of talk."

Out of the corner of his eye, Duncan saw the two homesteaders nervously look toward them then hurriedly leave the saloon. He also saw Wayne reach under the counter where he kept his short-barrelled Greener shotgun.

Duncan spoke softly and coldly, afraid he might have gone too far. "Sit down, Moe. There's a better way to take care of Mogan than bracing him head on."

Moe stared down at Duncan. His simple mind trying to sort out the facts. "There is?" he asked.

"There is. Now sit down," Duncan commanded, putting more authority in his voice.

Moe's labored breathing filled the room. He slumped heavily in his chair. "He's got no right to talk about me that way."

"If you call him out, people are going to agree with him," Duncan answered slyly. "Here's how to prove to everyone that what he says about you is wrong." He quietly outlined his plan.

With no one else left in the saloon, Gil Wayne had plenty of time to watch the pair. Moe's outburst, as Duncan had guessed, sent Wayne to his shotgun. During their quiet conversation he relaxed, but kept alert. Moe's anger seemed to have dissipated and as Duncan talked, Moe kept nodding his head. Although the switch was quick, Wayne did not miss it. Duncan had slipped Cotter his pearl-handled .41 Colt.

Kerosene lamps in the sunbeaten buildings of the frontier town were throwing shadows of pale yellow light onto the street as storekeepers locked their shops for the night.

Frank Mogan had left town to care for the stock at their ranch. Mike Mogan was making the rounds of the saloons. His earlier frame of mind tempered as his drinking increased. With Frank gone, he had no one to help fuel his earlier anger.

He was in a more peaceful frame of mind, and mellowed by alcohol, when Moe Cotter stepped out of a shadowed alley to greet him. "Howdy, Mike," Cotter said affably, poking back his Stetson with a dirty, broken-nailed thumb. "Haven't seen you in a spell."

Mogan stopped, examined Moe, then a half-smile crossed his face. He had not noticed Moe in the cafe, so intense was his anger. "Guess not, Moe. What have you been up to?"

"Here and there mostly. Right now I'm headed for Graham's and a little stud. Bunch of the boys are starting a game. Want to join in?" he added, almost too eagerly.

"Guess not. Thought I'd get a bite to eat at The Antler, then head for home."

Mogan had no more than finished speaking when Sam Richards, the newly appointed County Clerk, came from behind and slapped him on the back. "Understand you and Frank are unhappy about the permits," he said jovially. "How about a drink and let's talk it over."

Mogan hesitated, and drew back. "Guess not."

Richards insisted. "It's on me. Maybe we can make an exception on those permits."

Before Mogan could answer, Richards locked his arm around the half-sober rancher and steered him toward the saloon. Cotter followed closely behind.

Once inside, Cotter flanked Mogan and they crowded him toward a table in the corner.

"Might as well play a few hands while we have our drink. Afterwards we can talk," said Richards. He nodded at two men who were already seated; Charley Conwell and a man Mogan recognized as being one of Major Duncan's drovers. They were dealing a game of face-up. Conwell glanced up. "Hello Mike," he said coldly.

Mogan started to draw back, but bumped into Moe. "Guess I'll pass on the cards. I . . . "

Before he could finish, Conwell stood up. "Too good to play cards with us, Mike?"

A film of sweat covered Mogan's upper lip. He looked around the saloon. No one had noticed his predicament. "Maybe a hand or two," he stammered through dry lips. His voice barely audible.

"A hand or two it is," Cotter said, shoving Mogan into a seat.

Richards and Cotter took the two remaining chairs. Cotter directly faced Mogan, who, feeling a bump against his chair glanced over his shoulder. Another of Duncan's hired guns was standing to his left, blocking any exit.

The first hand was dealt. After the ante Conwell and Richards matched the bet. They both folded after Mogan's raise.

"Looks like you win this hand, Mike," Moe Cotter said, his voice getting colder as he picked up a second deck of cards on the table. "My deal this time and I call face-up show down. Five dollar bet."

The cards were dealt out one at a time. Mogan's first card was an eight. He paired on the second card. The third card was an ace, followed by another ace.

"Two pair, Mike. That doesn't beat Moe's three kings and queen." Charley Conwell's voice shattered the stillness that preceded the deal. "Let's see what the last card says, Moe."

Moe Cotter dealt, his eyes fixed on Mike Mogan. A third ace fell, but Moe didn't bother to look at it. He dealt around the table, deliberately and slowly. As he turned over a card for himself he glanced down. A three of clubs. Then he looked at Mogan's cards, then into Mogan's frightened eyes.

"Well, what do you know. Look at that, boys. Mike drew aces and eights. A dead man's hand. Isn't he lucky to be in the coroner's saloon." His maniacal cackle had a touch of madness as he drew Duncan's pearl-handled revolver from his belt and fired three evenly spaced shots into Mike Mogan's chest.

CHAPTER TWENTY THREE

The following day, after Frank Mogan heard about his brother Mike's killing, he rode furiously into town and drew up in a swirl of snow dust before Graham's saloon. Savagely jerking his reigns he yanked his horse to a stop so suddenly the animal settled on its hindquarters and slid, spraddling, into the hitching post.

Frank left the buckskin without a backward glance as it struggled to its feet and stood with legs spread, wheezing to draw air into lungs that desperately needed oxygen. The horse's coat was covered with a lather of foam.

Mogan knocked aside the swinging doors with the flat of his hands and kicked a chair that stood in his way. He walked the length of the saloon and entered the back room, where Graham did his undertaking work.

Dick Graham was standing by a newly constructed coffin, shirt sleeves rolled up, hammer in one hand, a fistful of two-penny nails in the other.

"Where is he?" Mogan demanded.

"You passed him, Frank. He's out front," Graham responded somberly.

Mogan whirled and stomped back. He had missed the canvas covered figure that was stretched over two tables placed end-to-end. He stopped a moment as if undecided, then threw back the tarp that covered the body of his only brother. Sightless eyes stared back at him. He turned to Graham who had followed.

"I was told Moe Cotter did this."

Graham nodded.

"Where is he?"

Graham swallowed against the hard knot in his throat. "Last I heard, he was in Kelley's bar."

Mogan stormed out. Before heading for the saloon he stopped at his spent horse and pulled a Winchester carbine from its saddle holster. Jerking it free, he levered in a shell.

The jumble of voices and blasts of laughter stopped as Mogan stepped inside Kelley's. He quickly glanced around. Moe Cotter was nowhere in sight, but lined up at the bar were Major Sid Duncan, Charley Conwell and the Duncan rider who had stood behind Mike Mogan at the card table. All activity in the saloon ceased as heads turned toward Frank Mogan.

Major Duncan stared hard at the murdered man's brother before he spoke. "Frank," he said consolingly. "We were all saddened to hear about your brother. You have our deepest sympathies."

"Where's Moe?" Frank Mogan spat back, his voice tight with anger.

"Moe? No one's seen him since last night. Have you boys?" he asked, looking around, first at Conwell, then his hired hand who stood at Conwell's side.

"Guess he lit out when he heard you might be coming in, Frank," Conwell said sarcastically.

"A terrible thing. Just terrible," the Major soothed. "Gives law and order a bad name. No hard feelings at a time like this, Frank. I'd be obliged to buy you a drink."

Seeing Mogan hesitate, he added, "Looks like you could use one."

Not knowing what to do next, Mogan lowered his rifle. He slipped the safety on and nodded curtly. "I guess I could."

Major Duncan made room as Frank Mogan joined him.

As soon as Mogan rested his rifle against the pine-fronted bar and placed both arms on the counter, Duncan took a step back, pulled out the same pearl-handled Colt he had slipped to Moe, and shot Mogan in the back of the neck.

As he pulled the trigger, he uttered an oath. "There's your permit. The same one your brother got."

CHAPTER TWENTY FOUR

The cold-blooded and senseless killings of Mike and Frank Mogan stunned the entire cattle-dependent community. Anxious groups formed in the streets, discussing the two murders and recalling those that had taken place earlier. From the pulpit of the Union Church, Clay Neese denounced the lawlessness that had descended on Prineville. Headlines in the Saturday edition of the *Ochoco Pioneer* screamed: **Vigilante Terror. Two More Die!! Who Will Be Next?**

A demand for action hung in the air waiting for someone, something, to set if off. Clay Howard dispatched a rider to the Triple C to let Tom know what had happened, and to tell him a meeting was being held that night at his home. Tom rode to town immediately.

It was a tight-lipped and somber group that gathered in Clay's sitting room and overflowed into the Howard's connecting dining room. Tom knew everyone there: Jeb Stuart; Sam Smith; Steve Staats; John Combs; Clay Neese; David Templeton, the town's only pharmacist; Isaac Ketchum, a local merchant; Al Lyle and F. H. McDonald, prominent landowners.

There was another man present. Tom tried to hide his surprise as he nodded to Bill Russell.

When his visitors had settled into chairs or sat, sprawl-legged on the floor, Clay went to the opening that divided the two rooms.

"I called you here, so I'll start the meeting. But I'm not appointing myself head of this group, nor do I think we need one yet. We're all individuals, used to making our own decisions and paying our own way. I think we should all have equal say. Anyone disagree?"

Clay looked around. Seeing no disapproval, and noticing nods of agreement, he continued.

"With that said, I'm opening the meeting for comments."

There was a pause as each man hesitated to be first, then Jeb Stuart rose from his sitting position on the floor. "I guess we have all been hoping it wouldn't come to this, but it's time to take a stand. We have already lost three people who should be here today: Al Schwartz and the two Mogans, mainly because we were willing to be pushed around."

Clay Neese raised a hand. Stuart responded, "Clay?"

T. Clay Neese, the preacher of the Union Church, rose from his chair by the round dining room table. "I don't see a good many you in church," he said half in jest. His statement brought some sheepish grins and a ripple of subdued laughter. "Unfortunately many of those hypocrites I do see, sitting there sanctimonious-like, are the ones causing most of the problems in the county. I just want you to know I intend to continue to preach against the sins of these people from the pulpit. I also want you to know that if push comes to shove I'm not above buckling on a gunbelt if stronger action needs to be taken."

Encouraged by preacher Neese's stand, David Templeton stood.

"I've been worried about what I've seen coming. I don't believe in violence, but I do know this. Every bully has to be stopped or he gets bolder. The more he gets away with, the more he pushes. The only way to stop the Association is to draw a line and take a stand."

The small-framed druggist took a white, folded kerchief from his back pocket and self-consciously dabbed at the drops of perspiration on his face and around his neck.

"If we do draw this line, we can't back down. Those who do will leave the others exposed and vulnerable. I'm willing to put myself on the line, but only if I know everyone else here feels the same way."

Templeton shifted his weight and looked down at his neatly polished ankle length shoes. Then he glanced up. "If they don't, then I have a wife and family to think of."

"Dave's got a good point," thundered Sam Smith. "How about a show of hands? Are we here to talk, or are we here to do something about that self-appointed group of thieves that call themselves vigilantes?" He raised his muscular right arm. "I'm in."

To a man, the group collectively and unhesitatingly raised their hands. When it became obvious the vote was unanimous, Jeb Stuart got to his feet again.

"My partner Claude Pett wants counted in, too. He'd have been here today, but Claude Williams brought in a load of wet grain that had to be milled before it rots." Stuart pulled at his suspender straps, which were attached to his canvas reinforced workpants. "We've talked about this situation a good deal, and now that I know where you all stand, I would like to offer our grist mill as a lookout station."

Each man in the room knew the Stuart and Pett grain storage tower had a commanding view of the community and surrounding valley.

"That's quite a commitment, Stu," said John Combs. "These so-called cattle association members operate mostly at night, leaving their skull and bones notes on the doors of those who won't join. I've suspicioned for some time that they've been doing most of the rustling, too, just to get people stirred up. If we can catch them at it, we could settle their hash once and for all." Shifting a wad of tobacco from one cheek to the other, he added, "I'm willing to volunteer some men to help keep watch."

136

"Me, too," Sam Smith spoke up. His offer was echoed by every cattleman in the room.

"As it was my suggestion, I'll volunteer to handle the details," Stuart offered.

"Boys, I think we're making some real progress," rasped Steve Staats. "As those of you whose cows have wandered know, I'm a fairly good tracker. The next time the vigilantes do their night riding and some cattle come up missing, let me know."

"Steve, that's a mighty fine offer," said Isaac Ketchum. "I don't know how my feed and seed store might be of help, but if it can be put to use some way, it's there for the asking."

"I guess the rest of us are willing to make any contribution we can," Al Lyle added. "We're all in this together. Put me down for a night a week in the watchtower." He grinned ruefully at Jeb Stuart. "After the big fire in town, I don't guess you allow smoking."

"Sorry, Al. Chewin' but not smokin'," Stuart replied.

"Put me down for a night a week, too," said F. H. McDonald. "Also", he added as an afterthought, "David Stewart my neighbor thinks like we do. Unless there are any objections, I'd like to ask him to our next meeting."

"Good idea, F. H." Tom Pickett responded. "I'd like to add a couple of thoughts. First off, we need to recruit more people. The more men we have backing us, the stronger we will be.

"And second, it's going to be necessary to keep our activities under wraps. If the Cotter gang or Duncan gets wind of what we're doing, our goose is cooked. We have to be careful who we approach, and anyone who joins us must be sworn to secrecy. Each and every one."

His next words had a chilling effect. "We're not back-shooters. And we don't believe in killing. Our opponent does. Any one of us could be the vigilantes' next victim."

Clay Howard knocked a dottle of tobacco from his pipe, then refilled and lit it. As his eyes roamed the two rooms, he could see that the meeting had reached its course. He exhaled a stream of smoke.

"It's plain to see we are all of the same mind," he said. "I must say we've come a lot farther tonight than I thought we would. Unless anyone else would like to add something, I suggest we go about our business and meet again a month from today. Bring anyone you think might like to join us, but bear in mind what Tom said. Right now there are only eleven of us. We still have a long road to travel."

As the group filed out, Tom hung back. When they were alone, Clay Howard led him to the kitchen for a cup of coffee and the pie Ellie had left for them.

"I can read your mind, Tom," Clay said as they seated themselves in the kitchen's straightbacked chairs. "You're wondering why Bill Russell showed up tonight. And you're probably wondering, as I am, why he was the only one who had nothing to say."

Clay stirred cream and sugar into his cup and took a tentative sip before continuing. "I couldn't answer that if you asked. I completely trust his best friend Sam Smith, who brought him, but in my book Russell's still a question mark."

CHAPTER TWENTY FIVE

Two days after the meeting at Clay Howard's home, an editorial appeared in the *Prineville News,* now the only newspaper serving the Ochocos and Crooked River Valley. The *News* had bought out the *Pioneer.* Bob Reich, former owner of the *Pioneer* was moving to northern California to establish a paper at Eureka, an area he felt offered him more opportunity and less personal risk.

The editorial stated that County Clerk Sam Richards had appointed a grand jury to investigate the deaths of Frank and Mike Mogan to "clear the air and prove the innocence or guilt of those accused of the murders." The article also stated the widow of Frank Mogan was suing for damages in the death of her husband.

Those Richards impanelled to sit on the jury were County Commissioner Benjamin F. Alben, County Treasurer Gus Brinkley, and Sheriff Norman Frazier. The appointments were officially approved by County Judge C. E. Duncan. A note from the publisher appeared at the bottom of the editorial:

> *Although the hearings of a grand jury are usually private and confidential, this editor has been assured by Judge Duncan that because of widespread community interest, full particulars on its findings will be released to the* Prineville News *when the jury has gathered and examined all of the available evidence.*

Three weeks later, bold headlines on the weekly's front page announced: **GRAND JURY ACQUITS ACCUSED. COTTER AND DUNCAN PROVED INNOCENT OF ALL CHARGES.**

Under a smaller headline that read: **New Evidence Proves Self Defense**, was outlined the findings of the jury.

> *A verdict was reached last week in regard to the shootings of Mike and Frank Mogan, prominent cattlemen from the Lytle Creek area east of Grizzly Mountain.*
>
> *After many days of deliberation, the jury found "not a true bill," which proves innocent the claims against Myron "Moe" Cotter and leading citizen and noted Indian fighter Major Sidney "Sid" Duncan.*
>
> *Sworn witnesses testified that Mike Mogan "provoked and bullied" young Cotter, swearing that he was going to kill him over a card bet that Mogan said Cotter had reneged on. When Mogan reached for his pistol the 17-year-old Cotter, afraid for his life, pulled out a cap and ball revolver and got off the first shot which killed Mogan instantly.*
>
> *Eyewitnesses further stated there was no foundation to the rumor that Mike Mogan was killed with a .41-caliber Colt. Experts said the confusion may have come from the fact a cap and ball percussion pistol and a .41-caliber Colt bullet would have made the same type of wound.*
>
> *In the case of Major Duncan, a clear case of self-defense was proven. Duncan testified to hiring the Mogan brothers when they first arrived in Crook County. At that time Major Duncan stated they were going by the names*

of Tom and Frank Page. He became suspicious of their intentions when they left his employ to start a fully-stocked ranch of their own under the names of Mike and Frank Mogan.

Major Duncan stated that on many occasions he expressed curiosity on how the Mogan's herd had grown so quickly when they did not seem to be buying cattle locally. When he directly inquired of Frank Mogan, whom he had known earlier as Frank Page, a threat was made on his life.

On the day of Frank (Page) Mogan's death, Major Duncan was told Mogan was in town gunning for him. On hearing this, Duncan testified, "I determined to settle the matter one way or the other upon our first meeting. The test came sooner than I anticipated. On seeing me in Kelley's saloon, he attempted to draw his gun, but was too slow and fell with my bullet in his neck."

Duncan said he was distressed about distorted and untruthful statements he heard following the justifiable defense of his honor, and backed up his testimony with witnesses.

Inside the paper, in small type and lost among minor news stories, a four-line item appeared:

Widow Receives Award.

A sum of $3600 was awarded to the widow of Frank Mogan, to be paid by Major "Sid" Duncan

No other explanation was given.

141

A second editorial, surrounded by a heavy black border, appeared on the inside front page. It dealt with another matter:

First sheep in Camp Watson area!!!!

This paper has learned that five or six small bands of sheep have been grazing in the Shaniko hills. The News *was notified just this week that another 50 head have been moved into the Camp Watson area on the old Dalles Military Road, just west of Spanish Peak.*

They are owned by Harold Fritz, a German immigrant. Our informant also tells us that Fritz plans to winter more sheep in these lush grasslands as soon as weather permits.

The News *also learned that the Mormon community in Idaho have made plans to drive vast herds of sheep into Southeastern Oregon this spring. Such a large invasion of these grass destroying animals would be unwelcome news indeed, and could lead to violent conflict between cattlemen and sheep owners.*

Opposite this editorial, on a facing page was another item:

Reported Appearance of Rosslyn Robbers

Word has been received that the notorious band of horse and cattle thieves operating under the name of Rosslyn Robbers have made their appearance in the Ochoco Mountain range.

The Rosslyn Robbers, so named because of their successful robbing of the Community Bank in the town of Rosslyn have, until this time, restricted themselves to the Lost Valley breaks, east of the John Day River.

If the Robbers are in our area, it is bad news indeed for the citizens of Central Oregon.

Often, their method of operation is to pose as honest cattlemen; their aim being to infiltrate law-abiding stock associations in an effort to gain control or be advised as to what action is being contemplated against them.

When asked about the robbers Sheriff Norman Frazier said he was watching the situation and working closely with the Cattlemen's Protective Association. He implied the Mogan brothers may have been part of the Rosslyn gang.

Frazier also stated the Rosslyn Robbers were often successful because they usually stole only a few head of horses or cattle, making the losses acceptable to the ranchers —thus not provoking them to action.

If the Robbers are now in our area, Frazier expressed the feeling that it was important for every cattleman, large or small, who operates in the Ochoco and Crooked River range, to join the Cattlemen's Protective Association. "There has been a lot of rustling lately, and a vigilant and armed Association is the only way to put a stop to it," Frazier stated. He went on to add, "Some people want to give the Association a bad name. In my opinion it is the duty of every honest cattleman to join."

The Prineville News *echoes these sentiments. If we are to keep the Rosslyn Robbers, or any other rustlers, out of our community we must organize and, if necessary, meet force*

*with force. We question the motives of those
who oppose the activities of the Association
and ask them to join in a common cause.*

Buried on the third page, under a headline no larger than the body copy, was a notation that the area was being plagued by a number of rabid coyotes, and that stockmen should keep their eyes open for these animals that are apt to attack cattle, horses or humans without provocation.

CHAPTER TWENTY SIX

The backroom in Gil Wayne's saloon rang with laughter. The occupants had finished their second bottle of the bar's best whiskey and were boisterously celebrating. A copy of the *Prineville News* lay open on a poker table beside an empty bottle of rye. A third bottle stood beside it, as yet unopened.

One of the dozen men seated in the room rose. "Gentlemen, here's to your health." He raised his glass and drained it, licked his lips, then wiped both sides of his wispy, blond mustache with a bent forefinger. His light blue eyes sparkled. Sloping shoulders hung below a neck permanently stiffened by the bullet that was still lodged in it.

"There's no question the folks in town, as well as the whole county, know who is in charge now." Turning to the man seated next to him, he said, "George, as my defense attorney you did an outstanding job. Right, boys?" he raised his voice to address the slouched figures around him.

George Cotter stood. "Major, I accept that as a compliment. It wasn't all my doing, though." He nudged Duncan with his elbow, conspicuously winking one eye. "The grand jury played a part, too. Take a bow, boys."

Benjamin Alben, Gus Brinkley, Sheriff Frazier and Major Duncan's brother C. E. stood. With grave faces they bowed from the waist and when they straightened exploded in glee.

The bottle on the table by the paper was uncorked and passed along. When all glasses had been filled, Duncan raised his own once more.

"This time I'd like to toast the new owner of that noble newspaper, the *Prineville News*. George Cotter."

"Thank you, Major," Cotter replied, standing again. "As you know, Ray Douthit and I both had a small interest in the *News*." He nodded to the copy on the table. "Up until today's issue that is. I now own it lock, stock and barrel. Or maybe I should say we, the Cattlemen's Protective Association, owns it."

Cotter raised his hand to quiet the cheers that followed. "And we're going to be expanding our horizons. The next issue will carry its new name—the *Ochoco Review*. Copies will be mailed to every legislator and person of influence in the state of Oregon."

Feet drummed and fists pounded the worn felt-covered tables. Charley Conwell stood, went to the door that connected the back room to the main section of the saloon and yelled out to the husky, mustached bartender. "Gil, better bring us some more whiskey. We're dying of thirst in here."

Wayne turned to the shelf behind him. He tucked a bottle under his left arm and, holding one in each hand, came from behind the counter and entered the smoke-filled room.

An arrogant voice greeted him. "Wayne, when are you going to let your true feelings be known?" It was B. F. Alben, the town banker and County Commissioner.

All conversation stopped. Wayne became the center of attention. Unruffled, he placed the bottles on the table by the newspaper and picked up the empties.

"You all know my position. I'm neutral. What you do is your business. What I do is mine. I intend to keep my nose in my saloon and livery stable across the street."

"Don't wait too long, Gil," Alben snapped. "Your nose just might end up all over your face if you land on the wrong side of the fence."

Wayne locked eyes with the banker. "Ben, I make my own decisions." He crossed his muscular arms and took a spread-footed stance. "No one tells me what to do, or when to do it. No one. I want that understood."

"Now, now Gil, there's no reason to get bent out of shape." Sam Richards, the county clerk, addressed the saloon keeper placatingly. "It just seems to all of us there's no reason to wait letting everyone know where you are going to place your chips."

"That's right, Gil," John Ericksen joined in. "We're all your friends. It just seems sensible you'd want to side with us."

"My position right now is behind the counter. And that's where I'm headed. If you want to drink here, you're more than welcome. Anytime. Same as anyone else. If you want to drink elsewhere, that's your privilege."

"Kind of testy, ain't he?" Richards giggled as their host stormed out of the room.

"Testy and proud," said Charley Conwell. "Too proud, if you ask me. I wonder how high-hatted he'd be if that fancy livery stable of his burned down."

"There are a lot of people around town who need taken down a peg or two," Gus Brinkley interjected. "Selling and Brown, for instance. They're telling people who come into their store that someone should run a slate of candidates against us in the elections next June.

"And then there's Bill Russell. He's been making noises the same way. He's had his nose out of joint ever since we did Lucius Langdon in. He claims he told Langdon he would see that nothing happened to him and it's still sticking in his craw that we shot him." Brinkley's voice increased in pitch, becoming shrill. "If he doesn't watch his step, he'll be going up Cemetery Hill feet first."

A derisive snort interrupted the frail shopkeeper. It came from Major Duncan. "Whose going to do it, Gus? You?" He asked disdainfully. "You sit in your store all day long, talking big, but when it comes to getting things done, who does all of the dirty work? Why don't you put your money where your mouth is?"

A death-like silence followed as every man in the room waited for Brinkley's reply. Instead of hearing Brinkley they heard an indistinct mumble from Charley Conwell.

"What's eating at you, Charley?" Frazier asked.

"Just thinking. About the fact that Selling and Brown's store sits next to Wayne's livery."

Missing the meaning of Conwell's remark, George Cotter rose to his feet. "Let's not get off the track." His fingers gripped the lapels of his black wool suit, a characteristic pose. "One reason we're here is to celebrate the justice of our court system." He suppressed a cynical smile. "The other is to take stock of our situation." He eyed Gus Brinkley. "Gus is right in one respect. There is an election coming up next year, and we can't take getting re-elected for granted. Governor Moody appointed us, but he won't support us. He's a Republican, and he owes no more favors to the Democrats."

Cotter turned to his brother-in-law. "Sam, what is your reading of our chances?"

Richards remained seated. "I would say they're excellent, George. We control all of the county offices and call the shots in the Cattlemen's Association. Now that you own the only newspaper in town, and have control over what is printed, I'd say we were in the catbird seat."

"How do you read it, C. E.?" Cotter asked the county judge, pleased with Richards's remarks.

"Same way as Sam does. We don't have any organized opposition to speak of, and with the Rosslyn Robbers around most folks will be more worried about their stock being rustled than getting involved in politics."

Ericksen interrupted. "What about this new committee we've heard rumors about? That some of the locals are holding meetings to organize against us."

"Probably just talk, or it would have come to my attention," Sheriff Frazier spoke out.

"Talk or not, we can't be complacent. We've got to keep our eyes and ears open," Benjamin Alben said.

"After what happened to Luster, Huston, Schwartz and the Mogans, nobody's going to stand against us," Charley Conwell scoffed. "Our next step should be to speed up the rustling problem."

"Crude, but probably right, Charley," George Cotter said.

"Probably right is right," Major Duncan spat out his words. "There's not one of us here hasn't benefitted from the stock we've taken. It's brought the Association new members, and has put us in a position of real power. Not only that, it's financed our efforts. Now's the time to go full-bore after those who haven't signed up. Once they're in the fold, we'll have total control of the county and everything in it. I say strike now and strike hard. The appearance of the Rosslyn Robbers has given us a golden opportunity."

No more needed to be said. The group finished their drinks and filed out.

The last two to leave were George Cotter and Major Duncan.

Cotter twirled his glass, watching the wet circles it made on the soft pine table. He sat the glass down and glared at Duncan.

"Sid, that was a foolish thing you did with Moe, knowing he is simple in the head. And worse, you did it behind my back. I defended you because it was for the good of us all, but I can neither forgive or forget what you've done."

Before Duncan could reply, Cotter rose and stalked out of the room.

CHAPTER TWENTY SEVEN

Wispy white vapor clung to the lower ridges and draws below the rimrock foothills that towered over Crooked River. Silently it shifted, changing form and shape as the cool evening air pushed the ghost-like mass gently to earth. Like free floating smoke in a light wind, the mist then disappeared, leaving no trace it had ever existed. Within minutes twilight fell, casting its grey-shadowed fingers of fading light along the length of Beaver Street.

Fifteen years earlier this street was part of Monroe Hodges original plat. Hodges, a cigar maker's apprentice from Philadelphia, traded a racing pony and a twenty dollar gold piece to Barney Prine for Barney's store-cabin and full title to the land Prine owned.

Hodges laid out a townsite and named it Prineville, to honor the man who first settled the area. He also named the street to the east, that ran parallel to Main, Prine Street. Barney Prine could have cared less, but Hodges thought the designations were fitting and proper. Two years later, Hodges built the town's first hotel and livery.

The street that ran East from Main and crossed Prine became Heisler. Named after William Heisler who bought six lots from Hodges in 1871 and opened Prineville's first general store. Heisler's General Dry Goods became a stopping point for the stagecoach that ran from The Dalles to Klamath Basin. Because the stage picked up and delivered mail, it was only natural for Heisler to become the town's first postmaster.

Shortly after Heisler bought his land, Monroe Hodges moved his family to The Dalles. The street that bore Hodges name eventually became Second Street when First Street was established several years later.

Clay Howard thought of Prineville's early beginnings and how he and Ellie had helped play a part in the town's growth as he and Tom Pickett trudged through a foot of snow to a meeting of the Citizens Protective Union, the name that had been chosen for their group.

"It's too bad Monroe and Barney didn't stick around long enough to see the town they helped create," Clay mouthed his thoughts aloud.

"Pardon, Clay?" Tom, who had been walking silently by Clay's side, replied.

"Sorry, Tom. I was just thinking about the people who built this town. Guess my mind wandered a bit." Chuckling, he threw his arm around Tom's shoulder. "An old man's prerogative. How about a late supper with Ellie and me after the meeting's over?"

"Thanks, Clay, but I promised Mary Kay I would drop by and see her before I returned to the 3C."

"Have you two decided when you're going to tie the knot?"

"We're thinking about getting married the end of June."

"That's good news, Tom. I'm mighty pleased. And Ellie will be, too, when I tell her."

For a full minute they walked in silence, then Tom spoke, his voice deep and serious. "Mary Kay means more to me than I can say, Clay. I never really felt this way about anyone before." He paused to reflect. "I used to be all tongue-tied and awkward whenever I was around her. Now, when I'm with her I'm completely at peace with myself and the world. I guess everyone must feel like that. About the person they're going to marry, I mean."

Clay paused before answering. A bitter tone tinged his voice as he recalled his daughter's bad marriage. One that ended in her death. "I guess you and I are both blessed. And so is Todd, your partner and my grandson. Unfortunately, not everyone can make that claim."

Their conversation ended as they stepped into the oblong block of yellow light that came from the open door of the Union Church, where the meeting was being held. Once inside they were greeted by preacher Neese. "Come on in and close the door. These January winds don't have any mercy on us skinny types." He slapped his thin shanks to emphasize his point. "Most are here, so we might as well get started." Neese ushered Clay and Tom to bench seats, like they were parishioners attending Sunday services. Seeing them settled he stepped to the pulpit.

"As this is my place of worship, it only seems fitting that I start off. I only have one request to make. This is a house of God. I will look with great displeasure on anyone who uses blasphemy. Now, who has something they want to say?"

T. Clay Neese looked down from the platform on which the lectern stood. The coal oil lamps attached to two wagon wheels that hung from the ceiling cast shaded spots of light over nearly fifty people, each reluctant to be the first to be heard.

After an awkward silence, Neese said peevishly, "As I've expressed before, democracy is fine, but in my opinion it's high time we chose someone to take charge."

A voice in the back replied, "How about you, Clay?"

"That's very flattering, but my primary responsibility is to this church. I respectfully decline."

"I suggest F. H. McDonald," Al Lyle, McDonald's friend and neighbor spoke out.

"How about Bill Russell?" Sam Smith proposed.

"Two outstanding choices," said Neese. "Any others?"

"I think Tom Pickett would be a good man," John Combs said. "I nominate Tom."

Pickett stood, dropped his hat on the hard plank seat, and faced the crowd. "It's an honor to be nominated, John. Thank you. But I'm too far out of town to keep in touch on a regular basis. It would make more sense to choose somebody who lives here in town. Seems to me either Bill or F. H. could do the job. I move the nominations be closed." Tom picked up his hat and sat down. Clay gave him a questioning look as he mouthed the word "Russell?"

Tom took a stub of pencil from his vest and a slip of paper from his shirt pocket. He wrote the words "trust me" and handed the paper to Clay who read the message and shrugged in compliance.

"McDonald and Russell it is then, unless there are any other nominations." Neese looked around the room. "Being none, would the two nominees please wait outside while we take a vote?"

When they left, Neese said, "Let's get right to it before them fellas freeze to death. We'll vote in order of nomination. All those in favor of McDonald raise their hand." Twenty-three hands went up and were counted.

"All those for Bill Russell." Twenty-eight hands were raised and counted.

"Let 'em in," Neese said. "And give the winner the bad news that he's been elected."

Russell walked to the stage, shook hands with Neese and stood straight and tall, the posture of a man who has spent his life in the saddle. His ham-like fists gripped the lectern so hard his knuckles turned white. His tight lips broke into a slight smile, then resumed their usual grim expression. His huge ears framed his craggy, homely face.

"Never thought I'd be standing in the pulpit at the Union Church," he began. "I feel more comfortable on my horse, or in a saloon with one foot on the rail."

He turned to Neese, seated in a nearby chair, to apologize for his reference to the bar. This brought a hoot from the audience. Everyone knew of Clay Neese's fondness for an occasional drink, although they respected the fact that he never drank on Sunday.

Russell leaned on both elbows and looked first at one face then another. "After what I'm going to tell you, you may want to take another vote. This has been on my conscience for a long time. I'll make it short."

Squaring his shoulders, he stood to full height. He swallowed hard. "Cattle ranching is my life. I began trail riding in 1866 when I was twelve. My dad and I pushed three hundred head over the Willamette Military Road to Sacramento. When I was fifteen I drove five hundred head from the Willamette Valley, by way of Sweet Home, to Wild Horse Creek near Umatilla. Later that year I brought a bunch of scrub cattle to Prineville. I fattened them up and took them to Chico. With the profit I made I bought the place I now own on Willow Creek.

"When I was twenty-five, my dad sent for me to come to Brownsville, where Sam Smith and I both came from originally."

Russell caught Smith's eyes for a moment, paused, then added, "Sam doesn't know what I'm coming to. When he hears the rest of the story, I hope he'll still be my friend."

Russell's sigh could be heard throughout the church. He took another deep breath and continued. "My dad wanted me to take four hundred and fifty yearlings and steers to Fort McDermitt in Idaho. East of the Cascade Mountains we ran smack dab into the Bannock Indian war, and to save our hides had to turn our cattle loose on open range. After the war ended, it took a year but we were able to round most of them up again.

"I'm telling you all this, because I want you to know I love the cattle business. It's my life.

"I was sitting pretty until the winter of '79. I guess a number of you who were here at the time remember it."

Long-faced nods of agreement followed.

"That winter almost knocked me out, but with my brother's help we held on. Through the spring and summer of '80 we worked day and night to rebuild."

Russell pulled a red bandanna from his hip pocket, wiped some moisture from the corner of his eyes and quickly replaced it. His voice cracked with emotion as he resumed.

"Most of you don't know this, but the winter that followed did wipe me out. I thought it was the end of the world. When spring came, what little stock I had left were either killed by coyotes or drowned trying to find food near the creeks when the floods came. That's when I met Hank Vaughan. He was in the same boat, so we turned to rustling."

A gasped curse was heard that the minister missed in his own surprise. Neighbors and friends looked at each other in stunned amazement. Then all eyes returned to Russell.

"We only took two or three head from any one ranch. We figured once we got started we would return in kind. We didn't steal from our neighbors. Most of our taking was done from the big eastern spreads near the Klamath basin and in the southeastern part of the state—around Harney Valley."

Russell nervously ran the fingers of his left hand through his bushy hair, then unconsciously popped the knuckles of his right hand with the fingers of his left. The sound filled the quiet room like gunshots.

"Hank Vaughan was a hardcase, I'll admit that. But he was a good friend, and he never cheated or lied to me. Hank and I paid those cattle back. And with interest. For every two head we took, we returned three, using saddle irons to burn in the owners brands."

155

Russell raised his chin defiantly. "In case some of you are wondering why I took Hank in and kept him on, that's the reason.

"I said I would keep this short, and I will. But there's one more thing all of you should know. Major Duncan found out what I was doing and has held it over my head ever since. The night Langdon was shot, Gus Brinkley tried to get my brother Joe to help hang Harrison. I didn't find out about this until the next morning. By then it was too late to do anything. But I should have stood up and said something at that time. Just as I should have fessed up sooner about my rustling activities."

Russell stopped and pointed out Tom Pickett. "The only man who has heard the whole story before is Tom Pickett. It has been eating me up and I had to talk to someone who I knew would keep a confidence. When I told Tom last week, he said I should bring it up at this meeting and face the consequences."

Russell's audience sat, frozen in their seats, struck dumb by the confession they had just heard. Snippets of hushed conversation started, then a murmur that led to a babble of over-excited voices.

One man stood and called out. All heads turned toward Sam Smith, who addressed Russell.

"Bill, as far as I'm concerned you have always been a square shooter. Now I know, without a doubt, that my judgement was right. It took a lot of guts to say what you just did. The past is past. It's what a man lays up for the future that counts. As far as I'm concerned, you're still my friend and the right man for the job we chose you for."

To a man the crowd rose to their feet and roared their approval. The row nearest Russell reached him first, to pound him on the back and shake his hand. Clay Howard was among them.

After this expression of their support for Russell, a voice from the back called out good- humoredly, "Now that

156

we know what we all suspected—that Bill's a born horse thief—let's get down to the business we came here for." A ripple of laughter swept the room.

T. Clay Neese stood by Russell's side. "Bill," he said, "the scripture says to err is human, to forgive divine. I guess we have a lot of divine people here who don't seem to feel we need another vote."

Visibly choked up, Russell spoke out. "Friends, I just feel as if a hundred weight stone has been lifted off my back. Bless you. You can count on me to do my best." He sucked in a lungfull of air. "So let's get to the business at hand. As I understand it, Jeb Stuart has prepared a report from the watch tower committee."

"That I have," Stuart said, leaving his seat and advancing to the elevated stage. He laid out his notes, took a pair of octagonal reading glasses from his shirt pocket, and began.

"Two months ago, Sam Smith volunteered to set up a watch committee in our grain tower. And he's done an outstanding job. At our last meeting I told you we had seen some activity by the vigilantes. In every case we weren't able to follow them. Mainly because we were too late getting organized and lost their trail in the dark.

"Steve Staats suggested we solve this problem by keeping some men handy with their horses saddled. This we did. At Isaac Ketchum's Feed store. In fact, Steve Staats has been spending his nights there for the past three weeks."

Stuart's voice rose in anger. "It's as we suspected. On three occasions we followed them and thanks to Steve tracked more than thirty head that had been taken from the ranches around Grizzly. Most came from the Keenan-Morrow and Circle O spreads."

Stuart held up his right hand to quell the shouts of indignation. "They ran the whole bunch onto the Wagner boys' pasture above McKay Creek."

Stuart's voice shook with emotion. "Even a knothead could figure out what they had in mind. The Wagners not only won't join the Cattlemen's Association, they have been actively opposing it. Steve and I figure the Wagners were about to get what the Mogan's got, then the vigilantes could show proof the Wagners had some rustled cattle. So we drove the cattle back."

"Good thinking, Jeb," Bill Russell said. "Thanks for the report. You fellas did a right smart job. I guess the question is, where do we go from here?"

"Where we should go is down to Gus Brinkley's store and get some rope to hang him and the rest of that miserable bunch of thieves," Sam Smith yelled back.

Clay Howard stood. The very fact that he was going to say something calmed the crowd.

"Going off half-cocked won't do any good. We now have proof that what we suspected is true. That makes it easier to do what has to be done."

"What is that, Clay?" A. C. Palmer, a townsman and recently recruited new member, asked.

"First we need to write up the Wagner boys incident, complete with witness signatures. Then much as I dislike it, we have to let them keep up their rustling so we can document more of their activities. Armed with real proof they can't wiggle out of by saying it's the Rosslyn Robbers, or someone else, we bypass our county court and take this evidence straight to the state's Attorney General.

"The other thing we have to do is gather more support for the Citizens Protective Union. Particularly among the merchants. We'll have to let them know it's time to take a stand and that they can't continue to have their bread buttered on both sides."

Having had his say, Clay took his seat.

"Sounds sensible, Clay," Bill Russell said. "Anyone else like to air an idea?"

"I would," exclaimed Myron Powell, another new member who owned a survey company. "Elections are coming up this June. I think we should start campaigning now to get people into county office that don't just give lip service to law and order. Last year's trial of Moe Cotter and Major Duncan was a joke."

Cries of "Hear, hear," bounced off the rafters of the church ceiling.

P. J. Bushnell, another new member, rose. "I go along with what both Clay and Myron say. So much so, I'll volunteer to visit all of Prineville's storekeepers who are still sitting on the fence."

Bill Russell's eyes gleamed. "And, by damn, I'll go along with you, P. J."

"So will I," shouted Jeb Stuart.

"Count me in, too," yelled John Combs.

"Before this meeting comes to a close," said Dave Templeton, "I think you all should know one of Major Duncan's hands was in my store last week to get some tincture of laudanum for his boils. He happened to mention the vigilantes were aware they were being followed. He said Duncan called them Moonlighters as he doubted whether they could find their way in the dark without light from the moon helping them."

"By now Cotter, Duncan and their whole bunch must know we've organized to oppose them. But they're so brazen they don't seem to care," Russell said, pursing his lips and rubbing a day's stubble with a cupped hand. "Moonlighters," he mused. "I kind of like that name. Citizens Protective Union always did sound kind of fancy to me. What do you say? Shall we go by the handle of Moonlighters?"

His answer was a resounding chorus of whistles, cheers, stamping feet and cries of approval.

"Moonlighters it is, then," Russell said. "On that note I declare this meeting adjourned."

A bitter winter wind greeted Clay and Tom as they left the church. Tom shuddered as he pulled up the collar of his sheepskin coat.

"Feels like a storm coming, Tom," Clay exclaimed as flakes of snow turned to hard drops of hail. "Straight out of the Northwest."

"A little more moisture won't hurt, Clay. We'll need it come summer." Tom waved goodbye and turned in the direction of Senders' store where he was to meet Mary Katherine Reed.

Clay waved back and lowered his head against the icy drops as he headed home.

As Tom entered the general store, he reached up to silence the spring bell, an act which had gotten to be a habit. Mary Kay heard him open the door and rushed into his arms, hugging him tightly. The storm outside had arrived with full force, the sleet changing to a raging snowstorm.

"Tom, you must be frozen. The temperature has dropped twenty degrees in the last hour." Taking his hand she led him to the round, pot-bellied stove that was throwing its warmth around the center of the room. The lamp over the stove rocked gently as a result of the draft Tom had caused when he entered. By its light he saw a dark smudge on Mary Kay's cheek, near the corner of her mouth. He tipped her head slightly and affectionately wiped at it with his thumb.

"Ink. I see you've been working on the ledgers," he said. Then he kissed her gently. "Bookkeeping is something I always put off. When we're married you can handle that chore. What with the ranch, gold mines and shares in Captain Geyer's steamboat company, I really don't have any idea what my worth is. And a wife should know what her assets are."

"Tom, you're my asset. The only one I care about." She hugged him tightly. Reaching down, Mary Kay took both of Tom's hands in her own. "You must be starved. I've kept some supper warming in the oven."

They walked up the steps that led to the living quarters above. The homey smells of flour dough, cinnamon and stew filled his nostrils. His stomach growled noisily.

Mary Kay busied herself in the kitchen as he filled a basin with hot water from a large kettle on the stove. After washing up, he settled into the room's only easy chair and looked around.

"Where are Lou and Martha?"

"Lou had to take a load of goods to Tom White at Lamonta. Martha went with him to visit Mrs. White." Mary Kay turned from Tom to open the oven door, but not before he caught the deep blush that crept over her face. "They're going to stay the night."

After dinner, Tom stood by Mary Kay, helping dry the dishes as she rinsed and handed them to him. The newly washed smell of her hair and the warmth of her closeness made him giddy. As she dumped the rinse water into the sink and began drying her hands, he moved behind her. His hands encircled her waist and he pulled her to him. She moved against him, then turned in his arms to press her body tightly to his. They kissed passionately.

After a long embrace, Tom drew his head back. "I'd better leave. Wouldn't want to give the town gossips something to talk about, what with the Senders being gone and all."

"Tom, this may sound bold, but I don't care. What we feel for each other is decent and good." A shudder shook her slight frame. "I have had the worst premonitions lately that something terrible is going to happen. Something meant to destroy our happiness. I want to be with you tonight."

CHAPTER TWENTY EIGHT

Steve Staats stretched against his saddle's cantle to ease the weariness in his back as he turned down the trail that led to his single-room cabin. It had been a long night and he was tired to the bone. Since midnight he had been trailing four vigilantes. Where Bear Creek met Crooked River, just south of the Maury Mountains, the men he was following efficiently cut eight horses from Bill Tackman's W bar T spread and pushed them toward Hampton Buttes and the desert flats.

Staats didn't need to see any more. He reined his horse around and returned home. As he leaned over his sorrel to release the latch on his gate, the first hint of dawn broke over the Ochoco range, softening the harsh peaks of Lookout and Round mountains and erasing the dark shadows that hung in the bleak land he had just passed through.

Staats settled his hat and paused to roll and light a cigarette. Squinting against the smoke, a slight movement on his front porch caught his eye. It was no more than a flutter, but it brought him fully alert. Glancing down at the dew-covered road, Staats noticed a set of shod tracks that led to his home, then back out the gate.

He dismounted and examined them. Impressions in the soft spring soil indicated a large horse and heavy rider. Staats remounted and swung right to follow them, ignoring what had caught his attention by the door. Half an hour later he stopped at the rimrock vantage point that overlooked Prineville and Crooked River. The tracks he had been following merged with the well-travelled trail that led down the rocky lava slope to town.

Staats removed his hat and ran his fingers through his matted hair, kneading his scalp in the process. A look of curiosity crossed his face as he wondered who might have stopped by. The freshness of the imprints told him they had been made less than an hour ago.

With the full glare of the morning sun at his back, Steve Staats turned his horse for home once more.

Pausing at his gate to examine and memorize the shape and contour of the tracks, he led his horse to the barn, stripped the saddle and filled a nose-feeder with grain. He slipped the feeder over the animal's ears, patted the gelding affectionately on the neck and picked up a grooming brush.

After taking care of his mount, Staats headed for the back door, stopping as he remembered the slight movement that had caught his eye before he spotted the tracks. Maybe a piece of tumbleweed that had been trapped, he mused. Or even the movement of a sage rat. Now that spring weather had thawed the ground, they were beginning to stir.

He changed direction and stepped onto the front porch. Under a rock was a note. He reached for it, throwing the rock back into the yard.

The writing was almost illegible. Staats stepped out of the shadow cast by the porch roof and held it to the light to better see.

He grunted in disgust as he read, half-aloud, his lips moving as he followed the words.

Yur trackin days R over.
Git out of town or yu wil be ded

A skull and crossbones ended the message.

163

Angrily, Staats wadded the note into a ball and threw it to the ground. He uttered a curse. "No cowardly night riders are going to run me out of town," he told the silence that surrounded him.

Then he headed back to the barn to resaddle. Sleep was out of the question. He needed to see Bill Russell.

Russell was having his own problems. Just before dawn he was awakened by an insistent pounding on his front door. Groggily, he put a diamond patterned flannel robe over his nightgown, slipped on his felt slippers and, still half asleep, groped his way in the dark to the front hall.

"Who in tarnation is making all that racket? It's not sun-up yet."

"It's Bob and Pat Wagner, Bill. We need to talk to you."

"Now? At this hour of the morning?"

"We wouldn't be here if we didn't think it was important."

"Come in, then," Russell grumbled as he opened the door. "I'll stir up the coals and fix a pot of coffee."

The Wagners trooped into the house, following Russell to the kitchen where he lit a kerosene lamp, took the lid off the iron stove's fuel box, poked the remnants of last night's fire with a broken shaft of branding iron, added some kindling, and blew on the embers to get a flame going. Next he primed the handpump by the kitchen sink, drew some water into a chipped enamel coffee pot and threw in a handful of ground coffee. By now Russell was fully awake. He glared at the Wagner brothers from under bushy, unkempt eyebrows.

"Now, what's so confound important that you have to get a man out of a warm bed in the middle of the night?"

"It's what we heard last night, Bill," Pat, the oldest of the two brothers said. "We were having drinks at Kelley's.

Bill Stokes who works for Major Duncan had a snootful and was telling anyone who'd listen that he'd had enough and was pulling out."

"Pat," said Russell wearily, "I'm not much for guessing games. Particularly this early in the morning. What are you getting at?"

"Stokes said Brinkley was bragging about what he was going to do to you. He said they'd be carrying you up the hill to the cemetery, feet first. Then he said the vigilantes would take care of the rest of the Moon-lighters."

"Brinkley said that!" Russell's Irish temper ignited. "Where?"

"At a meeting the vigilantes had last night in Gil Wayne's back room."

Russell swung on his heels, jerking at the knot that held his robe together. "Have some coffee. I'll get dressed."

Minutes later he was back, his gunbelt around his thin waist, lantern jaw thrust forward. "You boys still mad about the stolen beef the vigilantes tried to plant in your herd?"

Curt nods and dark scowls answered his question.

"Good. Let's start getting even. I'll take care of Brinkley, but I need someone to watch my back. I suppose he's home this hour of the day," he added as an after-thought.

"Nope," replied Bob Wagner. "We saw him headed for the hotel cafe before we came here. Guess he's having an early breakfast."

It was full light when the trio reached the hotel. Russell entered the lobby and went directly to the dining room. When Brinkley saw Russell and caught the anger in his face he dropped the fork full of pancakes he was about to shove into his mouth. His face turned ashen. His eyes darted from Russell to the Wagners.

Russell took a spread-footed stance, arms hung at his sides. "I hear you've been saying things about me, Gus. Maybe we should have it out right. . ." Russell never got to finish his sentence. Brinkley jumped from his seat and bolted out the back door.

"Only thing out there is a high wood fence and an outhouse, Bill," Bob Wagner wryly observed.

Russell snorted in reply and followed Brinkley. As he sidestepped out the door, gun drawn, he gnawed at one end of his mustache, tense as a rattler ready to strike. Brinkley was nowhere in sight. A slight smile crossed Russell's face. He raised his pistol and fired through the half-moon over the backhouse door.

"Don't shoot," a voice shrieked. "I'm coming out. Here's my gun."

The door opened a crack and a pocket derringer landed in the dirt.

"Brinkley, if you don't come out with your hands up, I'm going to stuff you down one of them holes in that crapper."

Brinkley kicked the door open and emerged, hands high in the air.

Russell looked him up and down. "Gus," he said matter-of-factly, "you didn't finish your breakfast. As soon as we attend to that, you and I are going to wait for the eight o'clock stage to The Dalles. Then you're going to get on that stage. And if you ever come back, you'll be the one going up Cemetery Hill feet first."

As they entered the dining room, Russell saw the Wagner brothers positioned at opposite walls. They were facing George Cotter.

Cotter saw the murderous look in Russell's eyes and raised both hands chest high, palms facing out. "Bill, I'm not taking sides in this."

"It's about time you got some sense," Russell savagely shot back as he shoved a shaking Brinkley into the chair he had vacated minutes earlier. "Enjoy your meal, Gus. It's the last one you'll ever have in Prineville while I'm alive."

"Bill, I'm not really hungry," Brinkley's voice quavered. "Besides, I got to pack."

"Pack?" Russell replied angrily. "You're leaving with what you're wearing. If your landlady thinks you have anything worth sending, it will follow on tomorrow's coach."

After Bill Russell escorted the broken Brinkley to the stage and saw it leave town, he was told that Steve Staats wanted to see him at Stuart & Pett's mill. Sam Smith, Clay Howard and John Combs were there when he arrived.

Russell was still on the prod, feeling the affects of his encounter with Brinkley and show-down with Cotter. He forced himself to listen as Staats recounted witnessing the stolen horses and the note he found on his porch.

Clay Howard expressed how they all felt as he reached out and gripped Staats shoulder.

"Steve," he said earnestly, "This note isn't to be taken lightly. Don't you have someone in the Willamette Valley you can visit for a spell? At least 'til this blows over?"

"No one's putting a can to my tail," Staats replied hotly. "I'm staying."

"If that's your decision, Steve, then at least let us keep a few men at your place," Combs said.

"No one's going to nursemaid me, John. Now or ever. I can take care of myself."

"Be reasonable, friend," said Sam Smith gently. "It's not like you're being wet-nursed. It just makes sense. The vigilantes know we're on to them and what we've been doing." He screwed up his face in concern for the young, unmarried rancher. "The only way they can lick us now is to catch us one at a time and they can only do that if we're alone. Be reasonable," he pleaded. "You're miles from town and all by yourself."

Staats jaw jutted in defiance. He had his pride. His mind was made up and there was nothing they could say that would change it.

Shortly after midnight, the bell in the tower of the Union Church rang frantically. Aroused from sleep, people rushed to their windows to see a dull, orange glow fill the sky.

Cries of alarm filled the cold night air. "Town's on fire." The metallic clang of the pumper bell announced its arrival. A bucket brigade was formed and watering troughs were quickly emptied as handpumps on hoses to the river tried to keep them filled.

There was no time for conversation. Everyone's efforts were focused on putting out the fire, the one thing feared most in a town of weathered and dry buildings fueled by woodstoves and open-flamed kerosene lamps.

When it reached the intersection at Main and Second, the fire stopped. It had been fanned by a slight breeze from the river, but the wind was not strong enough to carry the flame or burning embers across the wide streets that had been designed for two passing freight teams.

An exhausted group of firefighters adjourned to the town's four saloons, none of which had been touched, to take stock of the situation. The fire had started at the Wayne Livery Stable and quickly spread to T. Bushnell's Harness Shop, a vacant store and Selling and Brown Mercantile.

"That's a run of bad luck for Chet and Dick," Bill Russell said, referring to Chester Selling and Richard Brown. "They lost most of what they had in last year's fire, now everything's gone." Clay Howard, John Combs and Sam Smith, who had gravitated to each other and had joined Russell in Burmeister's nodded their agreement. Grimy and smoke stained, the four men sat silently at a table waiting for coffee, too tired to reply.

Steve Staats burst into the room, his shock of black hair hung in disarray over heat reddened eyes. He hurried to them, motioned and croaked through a smoke irritated throat, "Follow me."

Without questioning his instructions, the four Moonlighters rose and followed Staats out of the saloon. When they reached the corner of the livery stable, where the fire had started, Staats pointed an ash blackened finger at two empty cans of kerosene lying on the ground. The smell of the pungent oil still hung in the air. Staats took three steps to his right and silently pointed again. Leaning against the wheels of a burned-out flatbed wagon that had been parked behind the stable was a scorched, rough wooden plank in the form of a grave marker. On it, etched with a branding rod, was a grinning skull. Below the crossed bones the letters R.I.P. and the date, 1884, were burned in.

"Arson. It was arson," Combs cursed as he stared first at the evidence, then at his companions.

CHAPTER TWENTY NINE

Two months after the Prineville fire another disaster struck. This time forty miles to the east—in Mitchell, the town that had vied with Prineville for the county seat.

Mitchell was settled in 1873, five years after Barney Prine opened his combination blacksmith shop, general store and saloon. The first business in Mitchell was also started by a blacksmith. And, like Prineville, Mitchell became a cattle community. Mitchell was the halfway point between Prineville and the Canyon Creek gold fields along the John Day River.

A stage ran between Prineville and Mitchell twice a week. It passed along the banks of Ochoco Creek, by Tom Pickett's 3C ranch and the mines at Scissors Creek to the tortuous half-road, half-trail that thrust through the Ochoco Mountains to the flats beyond.

Mitchell was built alongside a gorge that stretched up from the banks of Bridge Creek. The town was located at the canyon's narrowest point.

Early in the morning, on the second of June, a gentle warm rain began to fall. It rained throughout the morning and into the early afternoon, increasing in tempo as turbulent clouds boiled high in the sky to the southwest. By mid-afternoon, an inky blackness covered the sun. Lightning flashed as roofs were torn from buildings by eighty mile an hour winds. Worried residents fled from the natural trough in which the town was located to the flats above.

Hail the size of marbles began to fall, forcing those who were scrambling up the steep-walled slopes to find whatever shelter they could: trees, fissures in the rock, outcroppings—even chicken houses. Many families were separated and the screams of frightened children were lost to the banshee winds.

Lightning continued to strike with vicious intensity, killing and burning to char exposed cattle and horses. The numerous twenty-foot wide irrigation ditches the settlers had built to water their crops soon began to overflow. Bridge Creek swelled in size until it stretched three hundred feet wide. The tremor its flow caused encouraged those on higher ground, who had remained with their homes, to flee like their neighbors below. They left just minutes before a giant wall of water tore through the canyon, its level reaching the top of the bluff where the terrified residents huddled and prayed.

The water carried huge boulders and giant trees that tore houses and businesses from their rock foundations, pushing them along in a flood of mud that had been washed from the desert. Beyond the narrow walls of the canyon, fences and orchards were covered with this ooze that spread for miles. Wagons, household goods and other detritus ended up as far as twenty miles downstream, such was the force of the water.

Carroll Wilson and three of her four children were caught in the raging torrent and swept away as they struggled up the hill. For three days after the storm had subsided, searchers probed the mud looking for them. Only the mother's body was ever found. It was lodged below a hundred-foot tall pile of driftwood, fourteen miles from the center of town. To retrieve the corpse, men lowered themselves on coils of hemp rope they had tied together. The three children were never located.

At Mrs. Wilson's funeral, a picture taken only a few months before, rested beside the coffin. It showed her standing proud in her best dress, a Bible clutched in one hand.

"Morning, Tom." Senders greeting was warm and friendly. He looked up from an order he was filling. His grey eyes twinkled over wire-framed half glasses as he lowered his head to glance over them. "She saw you ride in and ran upstairs to fix her hair."

A slow grin mixed with the sparkle in his eyes. "Been primping all morning, so I guess she won't be too long."

Turning somber he added, "Terrible news about that flood in Mitchell. A lot worse than our fire by far."

"Yes it was, Lou. Makes our everyday problems seem a little puny by comparison."

While Lou and Tom were chatting, Mary Kay came up behind Tom and gave him a playful poke in the ribs. He reacted by turning suddenly and she raised on her toes and kissed him fully on the mouth.

Taken aback, Tom turned a bright shade of scarlet. Mary Kay giggled at his discomfort.

Lou Senders laughed openly. "You better get used to surprises, Tom. Marriage comes full of them."

Mary Kay bent and picked up a picnic basket she had placed on the floor. She lifted the red-checked gingham cloth that covered it. "Smoked ham, fresh baked biscuits, spiced peaches and some of those bread and butter pickles you like. And," she carefully removed a napkin covered plate and held it to his nose, "hot out of the oven apple pie. Think that will be enough for lunch?" she teased.

Tom put his nose over the warm pie and with great exaggeration inhaled deeply. "It will be if we start with dessert first," he kidded back.

"You two have fun," Senders said, waving them off. He went back to the list he was working on. "Some of us have to work for a living."

Mary Kay bent over the counter and gave him a gentle kiss on the forehead. This time it was Tom's turn to chuckle as the cheeks of the store's owner turned a bright shade of pink.

Out in the street, Mary Kay took Tom's offered hand and rose primly to the seat of a buckboard Tom had brought in from the ranch. She left a full space between them, clasping her hands primly, back erect, as Tom touched a switch to the horse's rump. They trotted east on Second Street. When they passed over a hill and the last building disappeared from sight, she suddenly reached for the reins, pulled them out of Tom's hands and jerked the horse to a stop.

"Oh, how I've missed you," she whispered fiercely as she slipped into his arms. "I wish we were already married."

"It's only three more weeks," Tom said gently.

"Three weeks that is going to seem like three years," she replied.

"Well," he tried to sound casual. "We'll have to wait until we're married before we go on the honeymoon I've planned."

"Honeymoon?" Mary Kay looked puzzled. "Tom, we've never talked about a honeymoon. Besides, that's not important. Just being with you as your wife is enough."

Knowing her moods, Tom waited.

Mary Kay's mouth turned into a false pout. "I noticed you said the honeymoon you had planned. It seems to me you would want to consult your future wife about where she might like to go."

"Oh, I think she'll like to go where I'm thinking." Tom picked up the reins and flicked his wrist.

"Like for instance," he paused several seconds, "San Francisco."

He glanced out of the corner of his eyes, but was completely unprepared for what came next.

"Oh, Tom. Do you mean it?" she squealed in delight as she threw herself on him. "Are we really going to San Francisco?"

Tom pulled the horse to a stop once more, regained his balance, and tied the reins to the brake.

"If you would like. I've already made arrangements with my partner Todd. He is renting the honeymoon suite at the Palace Hotel. He and Ann want to take us to all the fancy social affairs. Of course," he went on, provoking her, "if you don't like the arrangements I've made," he emphasized the words 'I've made', "we don't have to go."

She stood and pounded him with both fists, making the buckboard shake on its spring-supported platform. "Don't you dare cancel." Then she sat abruptly, a look of despair on her face. "We can't go to San Francisco, Tom. I don't have a thing to wear."

"Ann thought of that, too. She's going to take you shopping. My wedding gift is a brand new wardrobe, complete with all of the accessories." Tom took her small hands in his. "After all, it wouldn't do to have the wife of Tom Pickett enter the social whirl in anything less than the latest fashions from Paris."

Mary Kay was silent. Stunned at the news of such an elaborate honeymoon. Tom released her hands. "Anyway, we have three weeks to discuss it. Meanwhile, it's such a beautiful day I thought we might ride up to Steen's Pillar." He knew it was one of the spots she liked best.

They left Ochoco Creek and followed the rough wagon road that ran alongside Mill Creek. Mary Kay touched Tom's arm. "Look," she said, pointing skyward, where a flock of smaller birds were attacking a slow, lumbering crow. "How cruel."

"Not really," said Tom. "Those sparrows are protecting their eggs and young." Such it is with man, too, he thought to himself, not expressing his feelings aloud. Alone against the crow, the small bird didn't stand a chance, but by banding together they were able to route their enemy; much like the Moonlighters, who had joined forces in a show of strength against the vigilantes.

It was one of those perfect June days. The sun, directly overhead, added its warmth to their happiness and cast dancing reflections on the surface of the spring-fed stream. The horse splashed across a soft marsh and stopped in a pleasant meadow surrounded by giant ponderosa pine. On a hill facing them, a tall sentinel of stone towered over a grove of jack pine that clustered around its base.

Mary Kay clapped her hands ecstatically. "My favorite place," she exclaimed. "Free and wild as it must have been hundreds of years ago."

She spread the picnic cloth and they stretched out on the ground, enjoying the mixed scents of meadow flowers. Mill Creek gurgled lazily as it meandered slowly below the imposing pillar of rock.

"How long do you suppose it has been there, Tom?" Mary Kay asked inquisitively, looking up at the shaft of basalt that rose two hundred feet straight into the air.

"As long as this country, I expect," Tom replied, pulling her to him. "Tom Congdon, who studies these things, says it's older than the Cascade Mountain Range and might even be as old as the Rockies."

She leaned her head on his shoulder as they gazed at the imposing monument. "What it is," Tom continued, "is the remains of a volcanic plug that cooled before it had a chance to erupt. The less dense lava mound that surrounded it has eroded away over the centuries until all that's left is the core we see.

"Major Enoch Steen, who charted most of the military and wagon roads through Central Oregon, found it. He was separated from his men and spent a night here alone, near its base. About where we are in fact. It has been called Steen's Pillar ever since.

175

"Say," he exclaimed suddenly, sitting up. "All this talking has made me hungry. Besides, it's been a long time since breakfast. Remember your Chinook jargon? It's time to *muck-a-muck*."

"Yes I do," Mary Kay answered. "It means eat. There's *hiyu muck-a-muck*," she said, pleased with herself that she remembered the phrase that meant much to eat.

After lunch, Tom leaned contentedly against a comfortably contoured fir trunk. Mary Kay stretched beside him, her head on his lap. She playfully tickled his nose with a stem of rye grass.

"Don't you wish we could lie here forever, just the two of us?" she said, watching the clouds rearrange their patterns in the sky. Not waiting for a reply, she answered her own question. "I could. Here we're part of life and all it has to offer."

Rolling on her side, she rested, her weight on one elbow and gazed earnestly at Tom. She reached up and touched his lips with her fingers. "You mean everything to me, Tom. I couldn't bear the thought of living without you."

Tom took her fingers and kissed them gently. "Three weeks from now, you won't have to."

A shadow crossed her face.

Perplexed, Tom asked, "Is something wrong?"

"No, I just had the strangest feeling. Like we have been here before. Sometime in the past. As if we were reliving this moment all over again."

Tom felt her shudder. She rose quickly. "It's getting late. I'll rinse the dishes, then we should head back."

While she was at the stream, Tom folded the tablecloth and checked the harness. It was then he heard the scream. His heart pounded as he raced to the river. Mary Kay was on her back, frantically beating at a huge, frothy-mouthed coyote who had her by the throat and was shaking her madly.

Tom looked around desperately. Finding a stout branch he grabbed one end and ran to her side. His blows infuriated the enraged animal, who dropped its victim and grabbed the stick in a death grip. Tom threw his weight against the coyote and held his knee against the beast's windpipe until it stopped struggling. He hurried to Mary Kay and lifted her slim body in his arms. She weakly reached up to touch his face. He could barely hear her choked whisper. "I love you."

Fighting to maintain his sanity, he struggled against the numbness that gripped his body and carried her to the wagon, gently placing her on the back seat. Some instinct told him to bring the carcass of the dead animal, which he threw on the floorboards. The dishes and picnic basket were forgotten. He whipped the startled horse into a dead run, not stopping until they reached Prineville two hours later.

Tom pulled the horse to a halt in front of Dr. James Snell's home and shouted for help. Snell had arrived in Prineville the previous year, and was the town's first accredited doctor.

Hearing the cries, Snell hurried out. Tom lifted Mary Kay's limp form and, with Snell's direction, carried her into the house and placed her on the sofa.

"Coyote," Tom choked. "Had her by the throat. Must have been rabid. Its body is in the wagon."

Elbowing the distraught cowman aside, Snell knelt to examine the punctures and torn skin. Then he opened her eyelids with his thumb. Sightless violet-blue eyes stared back at him as he felt for her pulse; first on her wrists, then at the artery in her throat. Feeling none, he reached for his medical kit and pulled out a mirror which he held close to her face. The mirror remained unfogged.

He rose and gripped Tom by both arms. "You did your best, but it's too late. I'll examine the coyote. If it was rabid, this is a blessing. Nothing could have saved her. Rabies is a slow, painful way to die and there is no known cure."

CHAPTER THIRTY

News travels fast in a small town. Within the hour, Clay Howard got word of Mary Kay's death. He and Ellie left immediately for Dr. James Snell's residence-office, four blocks away. They found their guilt-stricken friend leaning on a wall in the anteroom. His hands covered his face as he wept unashamedly.

Ellie went to Tom, tears coursing down her own cheeks, and hugged him to her breast, unable to speak. Clay threw his bear-like arms around them both.

"Why, Clay, why?" Tom asked, his voice choking on the anguish he felt.

"I don't know, Tom," Clay replied. "Man is the only animal that comprehends death. Maybe that means something. Maybe not. I do know our days on earth are numbered. We never really appreciate what we have until we lose it. Come home with Ellie and me," he said gently. "At a time like this, you need to be with family."

Tom stayed with the Howards until the day of the funeral. Services were held on Cemetery Hill, overlooking town. Most of the community turned out, for Mary Kay and Tom were both well liked. The day was bleak and raw. Cumulus clouds boiled in the sky as thunder rolled in the heavens. A cold wind swept the open knoll. Preacher Neese finished his prayer and closed his Bible. His wispy grey hair floated capriciously, stirred by gusts of chilled air.

All eyes turned to Tom as he reached down for a handful of earth and threw it in the open grave. He was grim-faced and dry eyed. The clods resounded dully as they hit the pine casket.

Tom stayed only long enough to accept the condolences of those who had gathered by the graveside. Most just filed by to shake his hand or grip his shoulder. Little was said. The mourners' silence was an eloquent expression of their sorrow.

As soon as he felt it was proper to leave Tom nodded to Reub Hassler, who rode up with Tom's horse. The entire Columbia Cattle Company crew had come to town to pay their respects. As they left, Sam Smith eased over to the Howards. An anxious expression clouded his face.

"I'm worried about Tom. He hasn't said more than a dozen words since Mary Kay's death."

"He'll make it," Clay responded. "It won't be easy, and the hurt will never quite go away, but I know Tom. He'll do what he has to do." Clay's voice became hollow and his eyes took on a vacant look. "Until you lose someone. Someone you deeply love, that is a part of you, you really don't know how devastating it can be. Until then, when a friend loses a husband or wife or child we say 'I'm sorry' or 'Is there anything I can do?' Unless you have gone through this pain yourself, you can't fully understand the burden Tom is carrying. And the sad part is, no one can hurry the healing process. All we can do is let him know he is our friend and that we care."

CHAPTER THIRTY ONE

Two days after the funeral, Bill Russell rode to town with the news that Steve Staats had been killed at his Powell Butte ranch.

Word of the death spread like wildfire. An emergency session of the Moonlighters was called for three o'clock that afternoon. They were holding an open meeting and the public was invited.

By three o'clock, an overflow crowd filled the Union Church. Built for a congregation of sixty, the place of worship couldn't accommodate the horde that showed up. Those who arrived early took seats, or stood where they could find room inside. Others waited outside.

Bill Russell arrived a few minutes before the meeting was scheduled to start. He elbowed his way into the building and through the packed aisle to the speaker's stand. The babble of excited voices quieted as he stepped onto the platform.

Russell squared his shoulders and set his chin. "You've all gotten word by now that Steve Staats was killed. The back of his head was blown off with a shotgun. I saw him, and I saw the ones who did it, hovering around his body like a bunch of vultures."

"Start from the beginning, Bill," a voice shouted out from the audience. "Some of us just got the word he was dead, nothing more."

Russell licked his dry lips and gripped the lectern, his eyes blazed from the fire within him.

"Sid Stearney rode into town yesterday afternoon looking for county clerk Sam Richards. Stearney said he stopped by Steve's for a visit, then went outside to water his horse. Claims he heard a shotgun blast in the house and when he went to investigate found Steve on the floor with his head blown open and his brains splattered against the wall. Stearney swore it was suicide.

"Mose Sichel and I were in town when he came riding in. He told us what happened, then went to look for the coroner and Richards. We hurried to get our horses and rode out, expecting to find nothing at Steve's place but his body."

Russell's face turned even grimmer, his lips drew into a tight line. His next words were strained. "When we got there, we found fifteen to twenty riders milling around. Men we knew belonged to the vigilantes. Steve's body was not in the house as Stearney said. It was lying on the ground in the back yard. When I knelt to check, I saw the back of his head was missing. He had been shot from behind."

Russell took a wad of rumpled paper from his shirt pocket. "I also found this lodged between the step and front stoop." He uncrumpled a sheet of paper and smoothed it out with his oversized hands.

After reading the message Staats had received earlier from the vigilantes, he looked up. "Steve told a few of us he had gotten this, but he said he had thrown it away. It's solid evidence as far as I'm concerned." He continued, his voice rising an octave, "The vigilantes didn't see me pick this up," he held the note high, "but Charley Conwell, who was there, sidled over and told Mose and me we'd better forget what we had seen because as soon as Richards arrived, he would verify that it was suicide.

"When I saw the way the gang around Staat's place was eyeing us, I said to Mose, let's get out of here. And we did.

"Isn't what I've said the honest truth, Mose?" Russell looked down at Mose Sichel who was seated in the front row.

"Every word, Bill. I'll swear to it. No man can commit suicide by shooting himself in the back of the head. I was beginning to feel like we might end up a couple of suicides ourselves."

Sichel's confirmation of what Russell told them had an electrifying effect on the crowd. John Combs jumped to his feet. "What did our impartial county clerk rule?" he asked sarcastically.

"Just as you'd expect," Russell answered. "Said it was a plain case of suicide, witnessed by Sid Stearney."

A low growl of voices began, then when those outside heard Russell's recounting repeated to them, it became a deafening roar.

Several Moonlighters joined Bill Russell on the pine platform and engaged him in animated conversation. A fever gripped the room and held everyone in its spell. A fever fed by a lust for vengeance. Not only for Steve Staats, but for all of the innocents the vigilantes had killed.

Russell recognized this mood as did those with whom he was consulting. Nodding his agreement with the decision they had just made, he drew his pistol and fired in the air. The shock of the shot stunned everyone into silence.

"I'm told the vigilantes are at Gil Wayne's saloon right now, celebrating the verdict of suicide and planning their next move." He pulled at his gunbelt, struggling to control his fury. "George Cotter was heard boasting they were going to break the Moonlighters back. I say if there's any breaking to do, it should be by the honest citizens of this community."

A roomful of voices howled its approval. Russell raised a hand for silence.

"There are a few of us willing to put our lives on the line to end this reign of terror once and for all. If any of you feel the same way, you're welcome to join us."

He headed up the aisle, followed by twenty armed Moonlighters. At Second Street they marched abreast to Main. By the time they reached the Wayne Saloon, another two dozen determined men paraded with them.

When they reached their destination they stopped and spread out, facing the saloon's half-doors. At Russell's direction, six men left to cover the alley exit.

Russell stepped in front of the group. His deep voice boomed out, "If there's anyone in the saloon other than vigilantes, they better get out now."

Startled faces peered through the panes of the saloon's two dusty glass windows, then several occupants scurried out, casting nervous glances at the small army arrayed in the street.

Gil Wayne stepped out last. He took one look, removed his apron, laid it over a hitching rail and walked over to join them. "There are a good twenty of them in there, Bill," he advised Russell.

"Better odds than they gave the men they gunned down," Russell spat back.

"Duncan! Cotter!" Russell shouted. "You have just one minute to come out of there or we're coming in." He pulled out the Waltham pocket watch his father had left him and held it in an open hand.

"Come on, Bill." Russell recognized the voice as that of Major Duncan. "Your men don't have the sand to buck us and you know it."

Russell glanced at his key-wind pocket piece and turned to those behind him. "That's it. Find cover. You're too good a target out here in the open."

While others scurried for protection, John Combs, Sam Smith, Claude Pett, F. H. McDonald and Clay Howard remained by Russell's side.

"Time's up, Major. What's it going to be," Russell called.

"Let's talk it over, Bill." This time it was George Cotter. "The six of you come on in. I'm sure we can hash things out."

"It's too late for talk, George. Besides, we'd prefer to stay right here. Where you can't get at our backs."

Five of the six men who stood facing the saloon drew their guns. The sixth, Sam Smith, pulled back the hammers of a heavy gauge double-barreled shotgun. The clicks of cocked weapons from those who had taken shelter echoed down the deserted street.

A curse shattered the tension. "All right. We're coming out."

"One at a time," Russell commanded. "Throw your guns and belts out first. Then line up on the sidewalk with your hands in the air. Anyone even twitches, we'll blast you all down."

The first to step out was Major Duncan, a sneer of contempt on his pock-marked face. He was followed by a more subdued George Cotter, then the rest of the vigilantes that had terrorized the county for the past two years.

Once they were lined up, Russell turned to F. H. McDonald. "Check inside would you, F. H?" McDonald selected three men and entered the building. They soon reappeared. "No one hiding inside, not even in the crapper out back," he called back derisively, a reference to Gus Brinkley.

The men backing the six Moonlighters had left their places of concealment and were facing their sullen captives, guns ready.

Russell faced Duncan. "Here are the terms, Major. You and your brother, George Cotter, Ben Alben and Sam Richards have twenty-four hours to get your affairs settled. Two men will watch each of you during this time. You will not be allowed to meet or talk to each other. The rest will leave town now. Any of them found in Prineville after an hour has passed will be shot on sight. Any seen in Crook County after your twenty-four hours are up will be gunned down without mercy. That includes the five of you."

"These are pretty stiff terms, Bill, I. . ."

"They're the only terms you are going to get. Take 'em or leave 'em," Russell snapped. "They're better terms than you gave Lucius Langdon, his hired hand W. H. Harrison, Sid Huston, Charlie Luster, Al Schwartz, Mike and Frank Mogan or Steve Staats. "In fact," Russell's voice turned ice-cold, "there are some of us here who hope you won't go along with them."

CHAPTER THIRTY TWO

There were no shootings, or hangings. The last of the vigilante leaders stopped, with one foot on the step of the Klamath-Eureka bound stage, to take a lingering look at the town he had once claimed as his own.

His wispy, Custer-style mustache stirred in the wind as he raised an arm to shadow his light blue eyes from a sun setting in the west. A look of defeat emphasized a large nose and ears that were out of proportion to a fragile face. He glanced briefly at the armed men who had escorted him for the past twenty-four hours, then at the crowd that had gathered to see him off. With a stiff-necked nod to no one in particular, he boarded the coach.

When the stage rolled out of sight, and only then, did the guards relax.

Sam Smith turned to his old friend, Bill Russell. "For the first time in a month of Sundays, I feel like I can breathe easy."

"We still have a job to do, Sam," was Russell's taciturn reply. "Not all the bad eggs are gone. Some ranchers in the Cattlemen's Protective Association think their membership gives them the right to kill sheep and sheepherders. And the Rosslyn Robbers need our attention. But this makes our job a lot easier." He forcefully spat a stream of chewing tobacco onto the ground to emphasize his point.

Clay Howard woke Sunday morning with a feeling of well-being. The scent of frying bacon wafted through the house as he bent over the crockery commode to lather his face. After he had shaved, he joined Ellie for breakfast.

Later, they sat together over a cup of coffee, each relishing the company of the other. Clay rose to get the pot and refilled their cups. Before he sat down, he leaned over and gave Ellie a peck on the neck.

"Why, Clay, what was that for? You haven't kissed me in ages."

"I know, Ellie. I didn't realize how much this vigilante thing has been preying on my mind." He seated himself, then reached over and placed his rough hand over hers. "You know I'm not much for showing affection. But then, after forty-five years I guess you've learned to live with that."

"Clay, you've shown how you feel about me in many ways. Words aren't necessary between us. You know that."

"I do know that, Ellie. At least I like to think I do."

They sat in silence, then Clay squeezed her hand before he withdrew his. "Let's go see Tom today. I'd like to tell him personally how we faced down the vigilantes."

Ellie bent and kissed his forehead. "I think that's an excellent idea. I'll bake him a pie."

CHAPTER THIRTY THREE

June, 1884

Lynn Wood was cutting John Combs hair when Jeb Stuart entered the barbershop.

"Come on in, Jeb," Wood called out. "You're next. We were just talking about the results of the election."

Stuart stuck his hat on a peg and sat down. "Couldn't be happier. With Bill Russell as our new sheriff and F. H. McDonald as county judge, I'll sleep better nights. I understand there was a ninety percent voter turnout."

"Not bad," Combs answered, "considering how far some folks had to travel to cast their vote." He paused to reflect. "Too bad the womenfolk can't vote. They sometimes keep us on the right course."

"Don't kid yourself," Lynn Wood interjected. "They probably influenced most of the votes, anyway."

"Well, be it as may, it's nice to see democracy in action again. Just as our founding fathers meant it to be," Combs said.

"Democracy doesn't come cheap, John," Stuart responded earnestly. "It's like the pioneers who settled this country. Or like building your own spread. Or my business. If it's worth having it's worth working for and fighting for. Nothing comes easy. Sometimes we have to start from scratch all over again." He paused to reflect. "Kind of like that Greek bird. The phoenix. Where the future rises out of the ashes of the past."

"I've seen mockingbirds and all kinds of jays, but I can't recall ever seeing one of them phoenix birds," Lynn

Wood interrupted. He turned to strop his razor. "Say, speaking of ashes, Gil Wayne tells me he plans to build a dance hall where his livery stable burned down. Now that's something for the young folks to look forward to, isn't it?"

Stuart's and Comb's eyes met. They grinned at each other. Stuart turned to Wood, suppressing a laugh. "Yes it is, Lynn. It's something for all of us to look forward to. And, as a matter of fact, I can't recall having ever seen any phoenix birds, either."

Author's Note

The Moonlighters is a fictional story based on the events and sequence of events that started with the murders of Crooks and Jory in March of 1882 and runs through the defeat of the vigilantes and the elections that followed in June of 1884. A violent period of two years and four months.

Many characters are fictitious. Two being Clay Howard and Tom Pickett, who are the glue that holds the story together as they did in *Wasco*, the book that preceded *The Moonlighters*. Howard and Pickett represent a composite of the cattlemen who settled in Central Oregon and maintained their integrity during the disastrous winters of 1879 through 1881 and the vigilante reign of terror that followed.

The dialogue is pure fiction, the author's version of what might have happened. Recorded quotes and statements that exist have been used, but even these could be considered suspect because record keeping in a remote frontier town in the 1880s left a lot to be desired.

Bill Russell and Major Duncan lived to ripe old ages and died peacefully. They both wrote conflicting and contradictory accounts of this period of history. Others were not so lucky. Charley Conwell was killed by a rancher after he threatened to take the man's rangeland away from him. Hank Vaughn was shot again at Athena, Oregon. He died years later in Pendleton after his horse fell on him. Moe Cotter committed suicide at a young age and George Cotter was shot to death in Canyon City. Gil

Wayne was killed in Harney County during an argument about a horse race.

I would like to thank Irene Helms, Director of the Bowman Museum in Prineville, Oregon. Without her patience, encouragement and many hours of research documentation, this book might never have been written. She likes to refer to *The Moonlighters* as "our book." She is right.

And thanks, too, to her husband Glenn, who was a pleasant and knowledgeable companion as we sought out and travelled the trails, routes and locations mentioned in this novel.

Martel Scroggin